PRAISE FOR
FLYING SOLO

In *Flying Solo*, Denise walks us through an honest and intimate account of the pain she experienced during her first year of walking through a divorce. She covers real heart issues such as learning to let go, getting through grief and disappointment, and allowing God to fill that secret place in our hearts that only He can fill. Although this book was written to bring hope and healing to those who have been through a divorce, I recommend it to anyone who wants to experience an intimate relationship with a loving God through every season of life.

Nancy Alcorn
Founder and President of Mercy Ministries

Flying Solo provides a companion for those going through the painful breakup of a marriage because Denise is willing to share the raw intimate pain of her first year of walking through divorce. Read it, do the homework assignments, dig in and make the most of your journey. Then buy a copy and give it to a friend, or use it in a study. It will open doors of honesty with others who have traveled this path.

Ken Edwards, MDiv, MA
Counselor, Coach and Consultant

It has been a privilege to look in on Denise's unfolding story. She lives as she writes, with authentic enthusiasm, exploring the collection of the moments we call life. *Flying Solo* is an invitation to peer into a love exchange—a soul environment between a woman and the One who loves.

Jamie George
Pastor of The Journey, Franklin, Tennessee

It is so easy when going through the emotional ups and downs that accompany the terrible process of divorce to feel alone and helpless. By sharing her personal reflections and her conversations with God in *Flying Solo*, Denise offers incredible comfort for those recovering from divorce and a hope for a joyous future. This book offers validation for the feelings we all encounter and a path of self-discovery that is uplifting, encouraging and inspiring.

Jenny Sanford
Former First Lady of South Carolina
Author of *Staying True*

There are few things that compare to the anguish of divorce. It is by definition a solitary and devastating trauma, especially for believers who honor love and the covenant of marriage. This book is a companion for those facing divorce, written by a woman who can testify that although weeping may endure for a night, joy comes in the morning. As you read this book, may God fill your heart with that same peace and hope He gave to Denise, which she now offers to you.

Dan Scott
Senior Pastor of Christ Church, Nashville, Tennessee
Author of *Naked and Not Ashamed*

Flying Solo

Divorce, Healing and a Very Present God

Denise Hildreth Jones

Published by
Denise Hildreth Jones
www.reclaiminghearts.org
Printed in the U.S.A.

Library of Congress Cataloging-in-Publication Data
Jones, Denise Hildreth.
Flying solo : divorce, healing, and a very present God / Denise Hildreth Jones.
p. cm.
ISBN 978-0-9889396-5-3(trade paper)
1. Jones, Denise Hildreth. 2. Divorced women—Religious life. 3. Divorce—Religious as-
pects—Christianity. I. Title.
BV4596.D58J66 2010
248.8'433092—dc22
[B]
2018903723

Rights for publishing this book outside the U.S.A. or in non-English languages are
administered by Denise Hildreth Jones
For additional information, please visit www.reclaiminghearts.org or email
info@reclaiminghearts.org, or write to Reclaiming Hearts P.O. Box 681526 Franklin, TN,
U.S.A.

This book is dedicated to my heavenly Father,
who allowed me a privileged season to "fly solo" with Him.

CONTENTS

INTRODUCTION

Grief has no etiquette. It is slobbery and mean. Obtrusive and inopportune. Smothering and rude. And it had taken up residence in every cell of my body. As I sat in the unfamiliar church that morning, it would offer me no wavering ounce of mercy. The divorce papers that would end my 13 years of marriage had just been delivered. Every part of familiar was gone. Today would be no different.

I had chosen to attend church that morning with my brother and sister-in-law. No one would know me there, and I would be given yet a little more time to absorb my grief in anonymity. The ability to process the weight of this extreme loss would be much easier with fewer questions and personal sanctuary. So, not telling anyone other than my immediate family and closest friends at that moment was the best gift I had given myself. Thus, the unfamiliar church.

The musicians began to play; the praise and worship music filtered through the dimly lit, makeshift sanctuary of padded chairs and tin roof. Candles flickered from every crevice and corner of the old factory, and wooden beams arched throughout the building. A young man sat on the stage that morning in front of a canvas, his paintbrush in hand; a spotlight lit the canvas as he stroked it with color.

Throughout the entire worship service, and throughout the message that morning, the artist worshiped. I watched each stroke through the blur of my own tears that had stained my face cold. At some point I thought the image was discernable, but I quickly refuted the possibility with, *No, there's no way. It can't be that.*

But as the final strokes were rendered, I realized it was *that*. It really was a man slipping a wedding ring on a woman's finger. It felt like a fist to the gut. The air was sucked from the room. The pain was bitter and mocking. My mind swelled with anger. There have been very few times in my life that I've felt truly angry with God, but this was one. And my anger spewed. *You've got to be kidding me!* my mind screamed.

Heaven gave me my moment. God graciously allowed me the rage of my soul. And when I was through, He spoke to my heart, *That is who I am to you. If you will allow Me, through this journey I will be your companion. I will be everything you need.*

My heart settled, and I listened. I knew He could be everything I needed. But honestly, at that moment, I just wanted my husband. I wanted the companion I had been given. I couldn't hold God. I couldn't touch God. I couldn't feed God my fried chicken and watch Him enjoy every morsel. I couldn't dream with God. A few days later, face buried in the oriental runner in my front hall, I told God, "Whatever you do, don't let my grief cause me to miss You." And that was the moment that heaven knew I was willing to let God be anything He wanted to be in this horrifically painful journey.

I had taught Bible studies for years on storms. I knew that often God was revealed best in storms. C. S. Lewis wrote, "God whispers to us in our pleasure. He speaks to us in our conscience. But He shouts to us in our pain."[1] I realized then that God has to shout in pain because pain screams. Pain wails. Pain is deafening. And I wanted God to shout. No, I needed God to shout. And shout He did, and has continued to do.

What you will read on these pages isn't the details of a divorce. It is the details of God in the middle of the pain of divorce. God "shouted" to me early on. *You honor the man who was your husband, and I'll honor you. People don't need the details of your divorce; they need the details of what I have been to you in the middle of your pain.*

He made this revelation even clearer when I was watching the movie *Out of Africa* on a flight back from Poland. Robert Redford's character had this old-timey, two-seater plane that the pilot flew from the backseat. When his love interest, played by Meryl Streep, flew with him, he had to look around her to see. But when he was by himself, he had a completely unobstructed view.

I've known for years that we can create monuments to our pain, idols that we coddle and caress, that we funnel our future through. But this was not how I wanted my journey to be. So I ran headfirst into healing. As I sat in a counselor's office only a few days after my husband left home never to return, my counselor encouraged me to do two things in this process of healing. Journal. Write as if I am speaking to God. And invite Him into this process. I have done both. Often.

For one year I chronicled the journey of my divorce and the beauty that pain can deliver. My journals, however, oftentimes held much uglier words than my editors allowed me to write on these pages. The rawness of my pain was far more real than words like "stupid" can portray. And, in all honesty, having to change words to appease book buyers felt less authentic than my heart can any longer be. That's why I'm telling you now.

Grief doesn't have a "religious handbook." As I said in the beginning, it is rude and, I'll add, often crude. But God is a beautiful companion to the companionless. And I've learned that God can handle even the ugly side of pain.

Although this is my journey, it could be yours. But let me say this, flying solo isn't about being alone; it is about living a life that may hurt at times, wound at times, betray at times; but it carries an incredible, unobstructed view of heaven and an opportunity to discover God in the middle of it. There is only one reason I would share this journey—wrapped in its rawness and digging into the deep places of my personal challenges, my discoveries and gut-wrenching heartache and then display it in black and white—and that is in the hope that you would have an amazing discovery in the middle of your own place of pain. Because God is in the middle of pain. Your pain.

God reveals Himself best in moments like these. My brokenness allowed me to see Him in the details of my life as I never had before, and though my ears never heard Him audibly, my heart heard Him over and over again. And I discovered that He can hold you. You *can* touch Him. He will love your fried chicken. And there is no bigger dreamer than He.

Note

1. C. S. Lewis, *The Problem of Pain* (San Francisco: HarperOne, 2001).

THE DAY I GOT
DIVORCED

Day 1

What do you wear to get divorced? That's the only thing that kept running through my mind. The sun was shining outside as beautifully and brightly as any other July morning that Franklin, Tennessee, could offer. But inside my home, staring at my closet full of clothes, the weather outside had nothing to do with what I was going to wear. Today I was looking for something that could be thrown away. Today I was choosing an outfit that I would never wear again, because it wasn't an event I would want to remember.

I ran my hands along the smooth fabrics of my pants. It seemed like every pair held a memory. A connection to a moment. Odd. I didn't know that I had memories regarding my clothes until today, looking for something that was expendable.

The soft blue polished cotton button-down hung with my shirts. I pulled the hanger off the rack and studied it. I hadn't worn it in at least two summers. It would be fine. I picked out a pair of black Capri pants that I hadn't worn in forever either. So there I was. Outfit chosen. Except for the shoes. I looked down at the floor of my closet and caught sight of the pair I had just bought. I picked up one of the brand-new shoes and simply told myself, *New Shoes. How appropriate. I am walking out of that courthouse into a whole new life.*

Then came the challenge of actually dressing myself. During the past few months, just getting out of bed had been a challenge. Some days, even getting out of my pajamas had been optional. But not today. Clothes were required for the courtroom. Whether or not I wanted to be there. I slipped them on and walked into the bathroom.

The mirror that ran from countertop to ceiling refused me the opportunity to avoid myself. I looked. My expression was foreign. How do you not know yourself? But I didn't. The look was so sad, so utterly sad, that I diverted my eyes away from the mirror. But I couldn't divert my heart. It was asking a thousand questions. *Is this what I'd feel if he had died? Will I feel this way forever? Can I die from something like this?* There was so much. Numbness. Dread. No matter how I wanted to look at it, it was death. What had begun with words of life spoken more than 13 years ago was today going to be pronounced dead. And part of me felt like I would die too.

I dressed in quiet. I tried to force my thoughts to pretend that this was just a normal day, that I was simply putting on makeup to run errands. I was applying lip gloss so I wouldn't look washed out. And by the time I was finished and slipped into the car, I had effectively made it through those agonizing moments without breaking down.

I drove down the street to pick up my best friend. My parents were back at the house, but she was the one I wanted today. And it was while I sat there, waiting on her, that You spoke something so sweetly to my heart: *Today is just the "legal" part.* There was something in that simple statement that allowed a spirit of calm to settle over me. I immediately thought back to my wedding day when we had signed our wedding license. There was no epiphany for me as the pen in my hand ran across that parchment paper. In fact, I think it was almost forgotten until right before we headed out beneath a rain of birdseed. My dad remembered, and we signed on the dotted line, legalizing our oneness.

But the becoming one hadn't been accomplished in my heart in that moment. The becoming one had begun two years earlier as we learned to love each other. It had been added to as we stood in front of each other and delivered our vows; and it continued as we became one intimately; and over the years as we dreamed together, cried together, lived together, fought together and loved together. All of those moments were what had created a marriage, not the signing of that marriage certificate.

The revelation that signing the divorce decree wouldn't mean my heart was divorced gave me the ability to endure the day. It gave me the ability to know that today was just a moment of the process—that over this next year You would heal my heart, piece by piece, moment by moment; and just as You had given me the ability to love to such a degree, You would walk with me through the journey of letting go. The journey of divorce.

Those words also allowed me to realize that the journey of divorce had begun months before. That even today wasn't the beginning of my *becoming* divorced. No, it began when my heart began to disconnect in order to survive. It began when I met with the attorney. It began when the divorce papers were delivered. It began the first night I climbed in my bed alone and knew that he was never coming back. And it continued each night after that when I would cry until I fell asleep with my pillowcase soaked. It had happened when my birthday came a couple weeks ago and he wasn't there to share it. When our anniversary had passed and the final year of marriage was marked in two separate houses on two different streets, living two separate lives. And it continued last night when I sat in front of my safe and pulled my wedding ring from my hand to place it inside a ring box and closed the lid with as much agony as if I had sealed a coffin.

I hadn't really even planned on doing it yesterday, but that empty ring box was just sitting there, and I thought, *I've got to do this eventually, so I should go ahead and have this behind me before tomorrow.* I got my ring from my jewelry drawer, and even holding it again felt like it was more than I could bear. I hadn't worn it in a while because I just couldn't keep looking down at it. So I had worn a simple pave diamond band he had given me four years ago when we renewed our vows. I placed it inside the box, but I couldn't close the lid. Because it felt like closing the lid to a coffin. And in that moment I knew that people, when walking through the death of a loved one, had to want to reach inside of the coffin and pull their loved ones out. Because all I wanted to do was pull that ring out and put it on my finger and live my life always belonging to this man. Always being his.

Every event we had shared ran through my mind like a video. The day he gave me the ring when he proposed. Our wedding day when I couldn't take my eyes off of it. It was everything I wanted. And for 13 years it has been a reminder to me and to the world that I belonged to someone and that someone belonged to me.

I just couldn't close the lid. I kept crying, aching over everything that closing that box meant. It meant I was closing the lid to my dreams. To the promises I had held on to, believing they were mine. To the miracle I had prayed for. To the covenant I had made. Placing that ring in that box meant my covenant was over. Over . . . never to come back. But I did close the lid. And today I closed another piece of my life.

Each of these events has been a piece in the redefining of my life. And that piece was just another step of the journey. There will be more. I know that. When I move from my home. When I have to separate furniture. When the only clothes left in the closet are mine. Each one of those moments will be another separation of two hearts, another part of the process of divorce.

But the beauty of what You gave me today was time. You removed the pressure of feeling that today somehow I had to act in a way that said the last 15 years were over and that I wouldn't feel anything again. Others may expect my heart to heal quickly. The unspoken thought, *You should be over it by now, because we are.* I know that soon people will move on. There will be no more questions of how my day went. If the tears are still falling, there might be a lack of understanding, a wondering why I "can't just let it go." But You have let me know with the simple statement, *Today is just the "legal" part,* that You will give me the time I need.

I know clearly that it will be intensely painful. But I have been released to not have to bear the weight of all the pain in this one moment. I have been released to take this moment, grieve it, see it for what it is, own it and then live through it. And just as signing that wedding license didn't cultivate a marriage, signing these divorce papers won't cultivate a divorce. Time will be what separates two hearts. And You will be what knits mine back together.

❋ ❋ ❋

Divorce has a lot of different faces. At least it did within the walls of the courtroom today. There were the faces of the attorneys. They lined the front row of seats like carrier pigeons waiting for their message. They laughed, they chatted, seemingly oblivious to the fact that for the next three hours they were helping to disassemble covenants as couple after couple would end something they had committed to cherish, to keep until death.

Then there were the faces of those of us behind them. Anger raged on the faces of some. Pain, undeniable, almost palpable, on the faces of others. Complete ambivalence on the faces of still others. My heart beat with an intensity I could feel pressing out of the ends of my fingers. When the judge took his seat, something in him reached me. He had a stoicism, a somberness, but he also had a compassion. I heard it in his first words to the first couple that approached the wooden lectern with their lawyers. Their faces were tense, their bodies rigid, their distance from each other less than three feet but as wide as a canyon.

They had been summoned with a "Smith versus Smith." This is what a marriage had come down to. It was now announced like an ensuing wrestling match. Some, I'm sure, had wrestled for months before they had come here. Maybe years. But an intense sadness swept through me. And it seemed as if I could see that same sadness on the face of the judge as he posed the question, "Is there any way you could work this out?"

I wanted to stand up and scream, "Yes! Yes, there is a way they can work it out! Demand it! Demand a year of intense counseling! Refuse to grant this divorce without it! In fact, why don't you remind them that they will now eat dinners alone. They will be the third wheel at the party. Some of their friends won't invite them over again. Tell them that they'll drive alone, ride alone. Tell them that one day they'll have to sit on the floor and pull out the drawer full of pictures and divide them in half. They'll have to take off their wedding band and never put it back on again.

"Remind them that if they have children, they will stand at the door as their former spouse picks up their children and they'll have no idea where they are going or what they will be doing; a piece of their children's lives will never be known to them. They will tend to homework alone, bandage skinned knees alone, take care of bath time alone, and discipline alone. There will be no breaks for hot baths or 15 minutes on the porch by yourself for a brain rest. And when holidays and birthdays roll around, there will be gifts you'll never see your children open. And when that same child gets married, you will sit on a separate pew from your child's other parent because of this moment, this moment right here.

"You will pack up the wedding album and memorabilia. You will pack up your wedding video and the Bible you received on your wedding day. But more than all of that, you will pack up the *what ifs*. The *what could have beens*. The faces of the children you will never have. And the 50-year wedding anniversary you will never celebrate. You will pack up holding that wrinkled hand on the front porch at sunset. And you'll pack away the ability to lay to rest the one person you had promised to love all the days of your life. So yes, Judge, there is a way. If two hearts are willing, there is always a way!"

But I screamed none of those words. I simply sat there quietly as the half-wooden door swung madly—entering the married, exiting the divorced—and then my case was called. I was now the "Hildreth versus Hildreth." Yet what those words signified, gratefully, my heart didn't.

I walked to the small lectern and met my attorney. It would be just her and me today. I had requested it that way. I had asked him not to be there. He had given me that, and I was grateful. The moment was as difficult as any I had ever known. It would have been made even more difficult by seeing the man I love standing next to me.

The judge looked at me so kindly. No condemnation. Just compassion. His questions were soft and emotional. My answers were whispered and wrapped in the strain of avoiding a collapse.

"Have all parties agreed?"

"Yes, your honor." My voice was barely audible.

"Is there any way this can be worked out?"

My tears rushed to the surface, and he became a blur of black. "No," I whispered.

He hesitated. I choked. "Then ... the divorce decree is granted."

I exited through that same half-wooden door, and it swung behind me, declaring this new station in life. The door felt almost mocking as it batted its way to its resting place. I walked out into the fluorescent light of the hallway and waited on my attorney to hand me the papers that would declare what had just happened. While I waited, I laid myself in Deneen's arms and cried.

There was something in today that I couldn't see this morning, but I can see now. Here was a judge, residing over the fate of my marriage, with a heart of mercy. In that moment, You gave me a reflection of You. Just like that judge's heart seemed to be hurting, Your heart, as my ultimate Judge, was breaking too. Divorce breaks Your heart. You hate it. And now I know why. I've read it for years, but today I know why. Because it is ugly, and sometimes vicious; it is always painful and almost always permanent. And what You join together You have asked man never to tear apart. But in the fallenness of us, in the casualty of divorce, in the pain of separation, You lovingly reside over our hearts. And You beautifully resided over mine this morning.

There is no protocol to divorce. There is no pattern of behavior. There is no guidebook that says, "On the day you get divorced, go to the courthouse and then hole yourself up in your house and scream and cry and cease living." So I knew that I could set my own rules for how I wanted to live out this day. And I did. Deneen and I met my parents and my sister-in-law at a quaint tearoom.

We relayed the events, and while we sat at the restaurant, I ate my meal and felt like I imagine someone would feel in a season of death—slightly numb, briefly aware and yet alive. I was still breathing. And I had survived this morning, which was something just weeks ago I was sure I never would.

I had been convinced that I would walk into that courtroom and run out the back door desperate to retrieve what was so lost and broken. But I hadn't. I had been bruised, but I was not broken—proving once again that Your Word is so true, when <u>You promised that a bruised reed You will not break and a smoldering wick You will not snuff out.</u> I had not broken, and I knew I was alive (see Isa. 42:3).

My parents and I went to the movies to see *Hairspray* that afternoon. I didn't know why; I just knew I didn't want to go home and have us sit there and stare at each other. And work hadn't been an option for a while. I hadn't written a page of anything since all this had begun. The only thing I had been writing was the chronicled journey of this nightmare. I watched the screen, the film characters moving about alive and full of color while my world felt as if I were living out a silent black-and-white film. Everything around me seemed colorless, as if there were one magic crayon in the Crayola box that brought all the other colors to life, but it had been taken out of mine, leaving only variables of gray.

When evening came, I slipped off the clothes I had worn to court that morning and put them in a bag to take to Goodwill. I put my shoes back in their box and declared that this was just the first day of a new life, then I put on a beautiful outfit, fixed my hair, freshened my makeup and headed out to my favorite restaurant in Nashville for a big dinner with my family and friends. The conversation was lively, and laughter was dominant. The awkward moment came when I shared a memory that my now former husband was attached to. I could see the shifting of the table, the slight uneasiness. I had gotten used to it, because I had seen it quite a bit over the last few months. But you can't move on from your memories until you have new ones in their place. And for me, he was a part of mine. There was nothing I could do about it until I had lived long enough without him to create new memories. Gratefully, everyone at the table respected my story.

When the young waitress came to get our dessert order, my brother looked at her and said, "Sorry, but we're going to Shoney's to get hot fudge cake." Well, the entire table cracked up. Here we were at this fancy restaurant, and this group of Southerners was going to Shoney's. The waitress looked at him and said, "I love Shoney's hot fudge cakes!" We offered to take her with us but left without her.

All eight of us cruised into Shoney's, and for almost two hours we belly laughed. I mean, we laughed from the deepest part of us. And for a few brief moments, I forgot that this had been one of the most horrible days of my life.

I walked to the side of the bed that had been my husband's for 13 years. I reached up to turn off the bedside lamp and looked down at the framed picture of the two of us that sat on the bedside table. It was taken four years earlier in Miami. It was a beautiful picture and was only a couple months after we had renewed our vows; the simple platinum band sat on my ring finger in the photo as a re-minder of that second commitment to love and to cherish. Prior to that we had been separated for six months and had come back together with what I thought was the beginning of healing and a covering of friends. Yet here I stood, staring at a picture with a wedding band while my finger was as empty as it had ever been.

I flipped off the light and climbed into the bed. Sadness swept over me. I think an element of my deep grief was over the fact that there seemed to be no road toward reconciliation this time. This really was the end. I looked up at the ceiling and began to talk to You, my present companion. "Thank You that I can feel You tonight. That You're here and You're mine. I'm going to need You a lot. I also need You to help me hear You when You speak and to keep my heart tender to Your tug. Don't let any bitterness settle in me, and please let Your grace continue to be as present as it has been each day, especially today. Thank You for today."

When I felt the assurance that You had settled over my heart, I closed my eyes and went to sleep. A life-altering day had ended rather sweetly.

MONTH 1

BEING FOUND

(AUGUST)

Day 2

There are stages to grief, and each stage demands the same decision. I made one today that I believe will change the course of my journey. My parents were still upstairs asleep when I got up and went to *our place*. It's the little path I made that goes through my foyer, into the dining room and around the front hallway, where I walk and we talk. As I began to pray this morning, I spoke these words out loud and with as much determination as any decision I had ever made: "Satan, you may have stolen my marriage, but you will not rob one more day of my life."

For the last two years, I had a women's Bible study for our city of Franklin, where I taught a series of lessons called Storm Proof. One lesson deals with how the enemy comes in and steals from us and how so often many of us allow him to continue to steal. When he comes in for the marriage, we give him our peace. When he comes in for our dreams, we give him our faith. *THE MESSAGE* says, "We make him our buddy" (Ps. 50:18).

But I knew one thing on this day after my divorce: I had no intentions of letting him steal one more moment from me. Not my peace, not my joy, not my future, not my expectations, not one day of my healing. It was a decision I made in that moment, and I set out to live it intentionally.

I am aware that I will still travel through the stages of grief. I know there will be days when I will be angry, but I am not going to get bitter nor live with unforgiveness. I know there will be more days when I don't feel like getting up; but I will get up and I will maintain my peace. I know there will be days when the tears will be far greater than the smiles, but I will still walk in joy. And I know there will be days when my heart will feel as if it is going to break with longing for my past; but I will maintain an anticipation for what You have for my future, and those are decisions I make today. The enemy will not rob one more moment.

How can a ringless finger feel so heavy? I kept reaching over in panic today, thinking that I had lost my ring somewhere. I stared at the white imprint where my wedding ring had left its stamp, wondering how long it would take until I could no longer tell it had ever been there. Only time will tell. Just like it will in so much of my healing. In the last couple of days, whenever I have gone out, I feel like everyone is looking at my hand. And my statement of belonging is gone. I have to stop myself with that thought. *No, the visible statement of belonging is gone.* But there is a place where I belong. I belong to my parents. I belong to my siblings. I belong to my friends. I belong to my shih-tzus. I belong to You.

I sat down on the familiar sofa. I have been meeting with my counselor, Ken Edwards, every week for the last two months. He was the second phone call I made after I called my mother. And next to my dependence on You, this is the best gift I have given myself. My demeanor has changed slightly since our first meeting. I can smile now. Talk a while without crying. The pillow still sits in my lap, but not clutched in desperation; now I hold it in comfort. I've memorized the colors on his tissue box, but I can make it about 15 minutes before he passes me one. We have come miles in the last two months.

"Tell me about yesterday," he said.

I did.

"You're doing great, you know. You're willing to push through the pain and do the things I ask, and listen to the Lord. You're doing great."

"Thanks. It's not easy."

"I know. But now it's time for you to start doing some of the things you've always wanted to do."

I immediately responded with that quirky smile. "Like ballroom dancing."

He nodded and smiled in return. "Yes, like ballroom dancing."

"I've wanted to take lessons for years."

"Well, it's time now."

"You think?"

"You could even do something crazier than that. You could take hip-hop or something."

My right eyebrow raised. "You've obviously never seen me dance. I could never do hip-hop."

"Why?"

"I'm the most uncoordinated person I know. Trust me, I can't hip-hop."

"I dare you."

I pursed my lips together. "Don't dare me."

"I dare you."

When I walked out the door there was something lighter in the soul of me. I haven't even taken my first dance lesson, but inside . . . yeah, inside, I am already dancing.

✳   ✳   ✳

There is a desire for the familiar in the midst of times of great pain. There is this seemingly innate desire for what you know. Yet, as I sat in my church this morning, I felt a shifting. Since I filed for divorce, I had attended another church. Not because I was running from mine but because I needed a season where I wasn't known. How crazy is that? I need a season without questions. So, I have hidden in the back corner of my brother's church for the last two months.

But now that the divorce is final, I am ready to go back to my old church, to what I know. Yet now, sitting in what I know, I sense a shift in what I need, proving that You never cease to amaze me.

In the middle of the greatest upheavals of life, You begin to purge things we would have never let go of. Places where we would have remained. And even though my heart craves what is familiar, what is known, You remind me in this moment that the only place I am truly known is with You.

Day 6

I didn't take my Bible to church today. I've carried that Bible to church almost every Sunday for 13 years, since he gave it to me during our wedding ceremony. But I couldn't take it today. I just wanted to get that first Sunday without it over with somehow. It's one of the last big things that binds us . . . that holds us together. It is time for it to go.

This was my devotion this morning from *God Calling*: "I am your Healer, your Joy, your Lord. You bid Me, your Lord, come. Did you not know that I am here? With noiseless footfall I draw near to you. Your hour of need is the moment of My Coming. Could you know My Love, could you measure My Longing to help, you would know that I need no agonized pleading. Your need is My Call."[1]

Thank You, Father. All it took was a need, and You arrived. Yes, I'm certain You have arrived.

Day 7

How can fear be such a motivator? In the middle of living, so much is missed, because fear is a masterful thief. It can be subtle yet intrusive. It can be veiled as self-preservation. Camouflaged as good intentions. And, at times, masked as mercy. But it is destructive and evil. And I had never realized how much I operated out of it. I am only now discovering how much of my action and inaction was and is largely fear-based. Fear of someone else's re-action. Fear of what I may lose. Fear of what I may discover. But as I was talking to Ken today, I realized that the thing I have feared the most is what I am living. And in the middle of that rev-elation, I thought, *If I'm living what I feared the most, then what is there really left to fear?*

I can't help but wonder if what You are allowing me to live now is forcing me to confront those fears. And honestly, as diffi-cult as it is to break these patterns of behavior, this cycle of de-nial, I have to thank You. Because until now I never realized how much of my life has been controlled by fear. Even as I'm walking with the pain of this divorce and the changing of behavior that it is forcing, I've fallen into a relationship with a friend that oper-ates in so many of the same ways as my relationship with my for-mer husband. And once again, I feel Your gentle tug forcing me to deal with what is simply wrong. Fear is wrong—as a motivator, as a tool of manipulation, as a means of avoidance. It is wrong. And it is no longer an option in my life. Yet it is interesting how I tend to gravitate toward this behavior. In a desire to keep peace I have denied myself. And in denying myself I am denying how You created me.

But in this journey I have asked not to miss You. And in not missing You, I also have to be willing to do the difficult things. I have to be willing to do what You've asked, whether that is cry-ing, getting angry or letting go. Today You are asking me to never again give anyone enough power in my life that he or she can control me by fear. Because if someone else is controlling me by fear, then my thoughts and actions are not being con-trolled by You.

So yesterday I found myself taking a huge step in a phone call I made. I had to ask some tough questions of someone I love. Questions I didn't want to ask. But I did. I asked them. So I know that You are helping me push past my fears. And I know that on the other side of all of this, I will have made huge strides in my own healing; and those patterns that held me captive are, piece by piece, being broken.

Day 9

There are moments in grief when you're certain that there are some things you will never be able to do again. Like get out of bed. Work. Hold a conversation without crying. And yet, little by little, moment by moment, You, in Your tender grace, begin to patch another hole. And today You did again. I was able to write today. And not just emotions written on the pages of this journal. But story. For the first time since all of this unfolded I was able to connect to that deep place of creativity and let the words of a story flow onto the page.

Six pages into it I realized that I *will* actually write again. Thank You that You don't leave me in the quagmire, continually floundering. But with each step I feel a little firmer. A little more solid. A little more sure that I'm not going to die. That You are moving. Working. Living in the soul of me. And that the gifts You placed inside of me haven't died. They may be forever changed. Strengthened. Wiser. Clearer. But not dead. And today I wrote. Today I realized that this place of pain won't claim everything forever. That as I am ready, You will once again return to me the things You've placed in my soul. And today it was a story.

Day 10

I can't get over Your detailed love. It started with my dog Chloe. When she died seven months ago, You did it just like I asked. I asked if you would graciously take her in her sleep so I wouldn't have to make the painful choice of putting her down. And one morning I went to wake her and she was lying there like a picture. But she was gone. And You let me know in the middle of that pain that You loved me with such a detailed love that You would take her just like I asked.

Today you did it again. I needed a new Bible, and I didn't have the money to buy one. At least, not the one I wanted. I called one of my editors at my publishing house and asked the price of a Bible that they publish that I had had my eye on for a while. I knew it was expensive but thought maybe I could get it at a pretty good rate. And today I opened the mailbox and there it was. My Bible. My Bible from You. It came with no invoice. Just a love gift. And I received it from You. My detailed Father.

In the front of the Bible I wrote my name, the date and who it was from. I wrote, "Your Loving Father." Because that is what You have been to me—a loving Father. And once again, in this seemingly simple gesture, but a lavish one to me, I hear You say, "I will not miss one of your needs, but I also won't miss your desires." You have so proven that, Father. Thank You for restoring to me something so dear that I lost.

You don't think you'll get epiphanies in the bathroom at Starbucks. But that's one of the beautiful things about You. You will speak anywhere I'm willing to listen. And what You said to me today has lifted another great weight off of my shoulders. The water was falling over my hands as I looked down at my empty ring finger. Separate from the extreme pain of not wearing it and the empty feeling of having it gone came this feeling of being exposed in some way. As if having that ring on all these years placed a protection on me. As if men weren't able to look at me.

And yet, with its removal it has felt like that hedge of protection has been shattered in some way. As if now it is okay to be looked at. Any time I've sensed someone looking at me during this past week, I have turned away instinctively no matter what his purpose was. Being looked at has felt uncomfortable and very disarming.

In your so gentle way, as the water poured over my empty finger, You whispered, "You don't have to look. You keep your eyes on Me, and I assure you that the man I have for you will not miss you. He will find you." I don't know how to explain what happened with those words. I've had no desire to look at anyone. But because of my people-pleasing personality, I didn't want people to think I was being rude either by turning away. With those words, You removed my fear of offense and you placed another ring on my finger—Your ring of protection. Oh, how You love me . . .

So tonight, as I came down the stairs of a restaurant in Franklin, where I'd just had dinner with friends, we walked past the bar to head out the door. I saw five or six men sitting there and felt that wave of nausea and uneasiness fall over me. Then I remembered. You don't have to look. You don't have to apologize.

It's amazing how quickly after losing your spouse your heart begins to ask the question, "Who will I get to love me?" "Who is out there for me?" Even though there is no desire for a relationship right now, and my feelings for the man that was my husband are still so intense, it is still amazing how the soul gravitates to its desire to be loved. I'm not sure why that should surprise me, since You created us this way . . . for relationship.

Yet, You have given me such freedom tonight. You have given me the freedom to love You, undistracted. Knowing that in Your perfect time and in Your perfect way . . . if You have someone for me, he won't miss me. Because *You* won't let him.

How many times have I watched *Diary of a Mad Black Woman*? But tonight I saw it differently. Tonight, when Cicely Tyson said, "God is a jealous God, and He'll have no man before him," I heard it. And I heard You. And for the first time, I realized that I had placed a man before You. Even though I have served You all my life, every time I let my heart get shut down, every time I quieted the gifts in the soul of me that You placed there, I was placing someone before You.

Forgive me, Father. Even though You have always been the love of my heart, I gave him places reserved just for You. I am laying down my Isaac. I am giving him to You, knowing that You are a far better steward of his heart than I ever could be. And all I need You to know is that I choose You. I choose You. Completely, totally. I have never heard You in the way You are allowing me to hear You now. And maybe that is because for the first time nothing is in the way of my heart or my soul or my mind that would cause me to miss You.

Day 11

I met with Ken today and there was nothing but tears. It's that perpetual displaced feeling. I told him about telling some friends the other day that it would be easier if I had just been widowed. Because then I could talk about him and share my memories, and people wouldn't care. They wouldn't get angry. I mean, I have angry moments too, but most of mine right now are just sad.

Ken leaned over and held out the box of tissues. He said, "I know you can't see it now, but this is a good place. You just need to rest in this place and not try to scramble to get your way out of it."

That is one thing I can honestly say I haven't felt the need to do through any of this. Probably because I'm too tired to even try. Even with my house on the market, I haven't felt the need to scramble. I'm just trusting that You know when it needs to sell, and You will have a home for me when it does.

"I do hate the thought of being divorced though, Ken. I have been so judgmental of people who have gone through divorce. I didn't think they had done enough. Prayed hard enough. Fasted enough. I'm really having to deal with the shame of that."

"Do you think there are any more judgmental ways about you?" he asked.

"Tons, I'm sure. I feel like I dealt with a lot of them a few years back when we were separated, but this is the one screaming on my radar right now."

He began sharing a story. "I have a friend who is a hunter. He can shoot with anything. One day an eight-point buck ran a doe into his back yard. He called to see if he could kill it within the city limits. They told him he could only shoot it with a bow and arrow. If he got it, but it ran to the neighbor's yard, and the neighbor saw it and claimed it, then it would be the neighbor's. So, he ended up shooting the bow but it went right over the buck, and the buck never moved because he was so tired. The next arrow got him, and the jolt caused him to jump over the fence, but he and his dad were able to get the buck before the owner came out. See, sometimes God has to kill things in us in order for us to become what He wants us to be."

I sat in that for a while. There was so much in it that I couldn't move quickly from it. "There is so much in me being killed, Ken. My ideals, my thoughts, my plans, my preconceived ideas . . ."

And now, as I'm journaling this tonight, I realize what You are truly desiring to kill . . . me. You are killing *me*. There is still so much of me in me. And I have no idea where we're headed. I feel that my heart has had a peek through the years, but honestly, from this seat in the stands, those glimpses of my future don't even seem possible. But I am learning every day that it has nothing to do with me doing anything but waking up each morning and saying, "This is Your day. My life is Your life. Do what You want today. Speak what You will. Use me however You desire. Send Your perfect people into my path and let Your will have its way in my life." This is where You are taking me . . . and I won't get there unless the me in me is willing to die. Completely die. So, yes, You are killing things in me. And the pain is brutal.

Day 17

I have gone almost a week without journaling. That to me is an amazing sign of healing, and something worth celebrating if just here on this typed-out page. You know, as people have started hearing about the divorce, and the questions have begun to come in, the only thing I have been able to say is how present You are. And as I say it, it seems to insinuate that there have been other times in my life when You haven't been present. Yet You are omnipresent. You are always present. But something about this situation has created in me this keen awareness of You.

And it has also posed the thought, *Does everyone discover this?* Why is it that desperate times can lead our heart in so many directions? I could have gone to a place of anger, and I've had those moments. I won't lie. Especially the moment before I had even filed for divorce, when I was in such a painful place that I screamed at You in the car. I screamed so loud. It was guttural. Tribal. Aching. Desperate. I blamed You. I blamed You for the entire thing. I asked where You were way back then. I asked You why You hadn't rescued and changed the course. And You answered me that day. So sweetly.

You told me that You give every heart everything it needs for victory. And whether we choose to grab hold of it or not is our decision. You don't make bad things happen. But You do show up in the middle of bad things. And I knew You had. I could see how You had. Allowing me that moment to accuse, to blame, to question removed my desire to stay bitter.

I had other options too. I could have gone to a place of despondency, to complete lack of care for anything. But from the very beginning, all I wanted to do was see You in the middle of this hell. And you have proven so faithful to reveal Yourself. It causes me to wonder how often I have missed you.

I'm not sure what has created this place of hearing You . . . of seeing You. I can only believe that it is You honoring my original prayer. I also believe that it is the complete place of dependency that my circumstances have forced me to, my dependence on You regarding my emotions, my state of mind, people's perceptions of me, my finances. In all of my years there have only been six months of my entire life when someone else wasn't actively involved in providing for me, on some level. And now, once again, I am brought to the place I was at as a young 22-year-old. Complete dependence on You.

Even though that is how You desired it before, it was not how I lived. I lived seeing someone else as a source of my provision. But You have shot that out of the water. And it is here, among the debris, that I will trust You. But do You know what is exceptionally beautiful about this season? It is the fact that it is just You and me. I need You so desperately, and I am finding You so personally.

I have known You as father. I have felt You as friend. I am discovering You as husband. And I am declaring that something beautiful is coming out of these ruins.

The mirror revealed something different tonight. It revealed a woman I haven't seen in a long time. I thought I had lost her. I had prayed and asked You to restore her. She is the woman of 15 years ago. She was full of life and her eyes danced. She was funny and could laugh from her toes. She had an innocent beauty and a quick wit. And she was gone.

One of my first prayers was to ask You to restore my youth. I felt as if it had been stolen from me on some level . . . years that I could never get back. Vitality and strength and stamina that I felt time had swallowed up. And so, when I was reading Psalm 103:5 the other day—"Who satisfies your mouth [your necessity and desire at your personal age] with good so that your youth, renewed, is like the eagle's [strong, overcoming, soaring]!" (AMP)—I claimed that as another confirmation of the prayer I had prayed.

And the face I found looking back at me tonight was so different from the one of only a week ago. When I look at old pictures, I hardly recognized myself. I saw a woman who was old, tired and weary. But tonight, that wasn't what I saw. I saw a returning of things I have prayed for. You really do restore even those things the locusts have devoured.

I've also sensed a restoring of my youth in how I feel. One of my greatest desires has always been to have children. Yet, as I've watched the hands of the clock swirl around, as if on speed, I have felt my strength wash away with it. And each year has brought a revelation that the "old gray mare, she ain't what she used to be," and there is a reason why You give children to the young. Yet, even that has shifted. Something in the soul of me is coming alive again. And I'm even feeling it in my bones.

I am coming alive! I feel it. And tonight I can see it!

Day 18

I came outside early this morning to sit by the pool. The silence in my house can be deafening at times, and I just want to hear people. To be around life. And there is life out here: the sound of laughter, women talking and kids splashing. It's just life. I had to come out early because the temperatures have been torturous. We've had an entire week above 100 degrees. As I was sitting here taking in the fresh air, just enjoying the beauty and warmth of the sun and the sound of the water and the peacefulness of it all, I saw such a paradox in the way the rest of the world is going. The stock market is insane. The housing market looks like it is about to freak out. And here I sit in the middle of this mess, and my own.

And then I pull out my devotion and read, "I come, I come. You need Me. Live much out here. My sunshine, My glorious air, My Presence, My teaching. Would they not make holiday anywhere for you. Sunshine helps to make glad the heart of man. It is the laughter of Nature. Live much outside. My medicines are sun and air, trust and faith. Trust is the spirit sun, you're being enwrapped by the Divine Spirit. Faith is the soul's breathing in of the Divine Spirit. Mind, soul and body need helping. Welcome My treatment of you both. Draw near to Me. Nature is often My nurse for tired souls and weary bodies. Let her have her way with you both."[2]

And oh, how she did, Father! Oh, how You loved me today in just the sweet warmth of Your sun on my skin. And You're right; Your medicines are trust and faith. Each day I have to go back to that. My trust and my faith and my confidence are in You. And in that I get some rest for this very tired and weary soul.

I made a huge step toward my healing this morning. And it came with an interesting revelation. I had to stop by his office today and see him. He was frustrated over something that had happened, and for the first time I didn't carry it. I even leaned back in the chair I was in and thought, *I don't have to make this frustration my*

own. And I felt the freedom of it. And crazily enough, I almost felt guilty for feeling it.

So when I had my appointment with Ken today, I shared with him the freedom of that moment—that I didn't pick someone else's stuff up as my own. And in that moment I realized how he had been on the throne of my heart. He had taken over all of my attention, even my prayers. I played protector, feeling responsible for his happiness and carrying his load. But I know I can't do that for anyone. Just like no one can truly carry this load I am walking through. I've had to seek You out for myself. I've had to listen with my own ears, allowing You to reveal to me one thing at a time. So I can never do that for anyone else again. I can't let my energy be consumed by trying to make someone else happy. I can love them well, and out of that happiness can't help but be a by-product. But to play savior is both exhausting and sinful. And I'm so sorry.

I honestly believe this is one of those life-marker kinds of days.

Day 19

I'm sitting in front of the movie theater and I've pulled out my computer, because I can't keep this emotion bottled up inside of me right now. I've got to get it out. Since I'm trying to get the difficult things out of the way so I don't live captive to my past, I'm hitting them head-on. And today is about going to the movies . . . alone. It was one of our favorite things. He'd get off early on Friday, and we'd sneak away to the early show and start our weekend a little earlier than usual. But today is different. Families are coming and going and I am sitting in my car fundamentally lost. The very basics of what I know are gone. The very normalcy of my life . . . over. Even what was abnormal had become my normal, and that, too, is stripped away.

I went to CVS to get a candy bar because I am fundamentally cheap and movie candy is outrageous and, sin or no sin, their prices are sinful. I got a candy bar just for me. I didn't have to wonder what he might want. I didn't have to pick up the phone and ask. And when I got the candy bar just for me and paid for it with the money that is just for me and got in my car with just me and went to a movie with people whose life is normal, it is all just me.

Families are coming out of the theater now. They're laughing. And it makes me wonder if I'll ever laugh that way again with my family. With my husband . . . my children . . . my family. I wanted all of this to be with him. I can't lie. And in the core of my heart I still do. I've released him. I have no idea what Your plan is. But there is still a huge part of me that longs for him to come home.

Today I am painfully aware that I'll never see a movie again where he is sitting next to me as my husband. Holding my hand. The nearness of familiarity. His touch. His skin. His smell. His shoulder—the one I've laid my head on a thousand times. No, I will walk into that theater and it will be just me, and I'll come out and it will be just me. Just like I got up and took the dogs out and took a shower and made the bed and cleaned the kitchen and it was all just me. And even as I'm writing this I know now why You said it isn't good for man to be alone (see Gen. 2:18). Because marriage brings two people together and makes them one.

How many times have I said, "Lord, have mercy, I would never go back to dating for all the money in the world." And yet now, there is the huge possibility that there will come a day when a stranger will be on the other side of my door, knocking. He will walk me to his car and open the door for me and take me somewhere and engage me in conversation, and I'll have to learn all his "stuff," and I don't want to!!!!!

I want what I know! Yet, what I know didn't work. It was so horrifically broken. And even in the midst of remembering all the broken places, I still ache for what I knew. I don't want to go in there, Father. With everything inside of me, I don't want to go in. But I have to go in to heal. Go in with me. Be there in the smile of the woman behind the counter when she takes my single $10 bill. Be there in the kindness of the guy who gets my popcorn and pours my one lone Coke. And be there beside me in the empty seat that used to hold a face and a name. This one is hard, and I need You desperately . . . desperately . . .

Day 20

There are moments in the middle of all of this that seem normal, that for one brief second make you forget that your world has officially changed forever and transported you to a place from which you can never return.

One of my first normal moments came two days after the divorce papers were delivered. I was standing in the store Bed, Bath and Beyond, waiting on a gift for a friend's bridal shower that I would attend with my mom and sister-in-law, Sarah. It was in the early days when no one wanted me to be alone, and so my family had converged on me. Here I was, staring out of the automatic-opening glass doors, watching the rain fall, and for one fell swoop I felt normal. And just as quickly as it came I remembered. And the pain fell as furiously as the downpour outside.

That moment was followed by an even starker reality, because the bridal shower was held at the same church where I got married. Sarah had never seen the sanctuary, so I walked her inside, and there on the stage was a young bride. The pastor who had officiated my marriage stood in front of her just like he had stood in front of me. Back then, I had held the dream of a perfect life like I was certain this young woman did. But standing there now, I just prayed that You would give me the strength to get through this life that is now mine.

We spent the next hour watching another young woman open gifts to take her to her wedding day, for a life she expects to be beautiful and perfect too.

A brief moment of relief came when we were riding the elevator down. It stopped on the floor where we were supposed to get off, but the doors wouldn't open. We all had a brief moment of panic. I said, "Well, wouldn't y'all love to be stuck in an elevator with a woman in the beginning stages of divorce." It was probably our laughter that finally jarred the doors open.

But then normal was decimated once again by a simple, everyday comment. In a world of abnormal, where pain is as sensitively on the surface of the skin as my dogs' noses are to the smell of food, the words took me to a debilitating place. My mom looked back at Sarah, the blinding rain still pelting the windshield, and said, "At least you can ride home with your baby and not have to drive in this weather alone." She said it knowing that my brother was waiting for us back at my house.

And in that moment I realized all the other things I would have to do alone. I'd already had the horrible dinner *alone* moment with my friend River and her husband right before the divorce papers had been filed. But in that moment I realized that from now on I'd be driving myself everywhere. I'd go home alone. I'd open my door alone. I'd climb in the bed alone. It would just be me. And when Sarah slipped out of the car, I fell into a screaming place of pain so deep and so physical that I could barely breathe. My words spewed out, not at my mother, but at this place, and I laid my head on the steering column and just let whatever needed to escape come out. And tonight was very similar to that moment. Tonight driving myself home, back behind the wheel yet again with no one to open my car door, slip behind the driver's seat and take me home, my grief consumed me.

There is so much comparison between divorce and death. I didn't realize it until now. But sitting in the middle of grief I don't know how you can compare it. Grief is simply grief. And for the one living it is the greatest pain he or she could know. I go back to the words I heard a family speak about grief one time; they said, "Grief never goes away; it simply explodes less often."

I wonder today if that isn't true. In those early days before my divorce, when the realization of where I was headed began to settle in on me, the pain was continual and unending. I'm nowhere near where my heart desires to be. There is still a continual hovering of my new reality. But there are brief respites from its explosions.

Yet this is my grief. It is my pain. It is unique. It is real. It is mine and I will walk through it. I won't run from this moment. I will cry through it. I will scream through it. I will yell through it. I will stay up through the night with it if I have to. But it is mine. And I am claiming it. And in claiming it I can heal.

Father, grant me grace. Grant me grace for this excruciatingly painful moment. Wash over me with Your presence. Sustain me with Your grace. And hold me in my grief. My heart is aching over what I've lost. My eyes are burning from the tears I've cried. And my soul is aching over what never had to be. But in this place You are present. And I will sit in the pain until this moment has passed, knowing that there will be a moment, and then another and another until I will have more laughter than tears.

Day 22

"Therefore your freedom will mean your rising into the realm of Joy and Appreciation. Clipped wings can grow again. Broken voices regain a strength and beauty unknown before. Your power to help other lives will soon bring its delight, even when, at first, the help to yourselves may seem too late to bring you Joy. Worn-out and tired as you may seem, and pain-weary, I say unto you. 'Behold I make all things new.' That promise shall be fulfilled."[3]

I believe that today, Father. And just as I prayed this morning that You would use me again, You give me a sweet word like this. So encouraging. So directing. So assuring. *Every* promise for my life shall be fulfilled. Every one. Not one will be missed. And the power in me to help others will very soon bring its delight.

Day 25

One of my friends came over tonight. She is going through a divorce as well, and has a beautiful little girl. Her situation has been so different from mine, and I can see her struggle. My heart was aching to be able to take care of every need that she has. I wanted to simply give her the money that she needs and wipe all of the pain away that she is going through now. But I couldn't. At least not in the way I thought. Yet, You allowed me the sweetest revelation of You tonight.

I'm standing there in the kitchen listening to her share her needs, and they were so big . . . so outside of what I had to give. So I simply asked her, "What do you need right now?"

She said, "I really need some dish towels."

I reached down into my dishtowel drawer and pulled out four virtually new dishtowels and laid them on the counter. "Okay, I have those. Now, what other need do you have? Right now?

"I really need a small vacuum cleaner. One that is easy to go up and down the stairs with."

I remembered that we had one up in his old office. I went up there and saw that it was still there. I can't describe the feeling I felt when I saw it. I pulled it out and headed back to the kitchen. "Okay, anything else . . ."

She looked at me oddly, but we were on a roll. "I really need a self-propelled lawn mower because I have to cut the grass myself, and the one I have is so hard to push."

I smiled. "I have one of those too. And I don't use it because the yard guy cuts the grass. We'll load your car up." When she pulled away I felt You whisper to me, "I'm going to take care of every need you have. Even your desires." And that is exactly what You did tonight. My heart's desire was to help her, to offer her something that would relieve some of the pain and help her see how You care for her. And that is exactly what You did. I have felt like I needed to guard the finances that I do have so I didn't feel like I could give those, but You still met her needs and fulfilled my desires.

I called her as she was driving home and said, "Do you realize what God just did for us?"

"What?"

I laughed. "He just gave you everything you need. He supplied every immediate need you had. And I wanted to give to you. So He supplied my desire. So, what do you say we thank Him?"

"I'd love that."

"Mind if I pray?"

"No, but I won't close my eyes."

We laughed, and I prayed. A prayer to thank You. A prayer to let You know that we noticed how You had shown up. A prayer to say thank You for caring about even our desires—our deepest longings that we don't even utter. You did that tonight, Father. You loved us both in our details. And I am so grateful.

Day 28

Why do we not give ourselves permission to heal? What is it about our design or our thought process that makes healing seem like something that must be rushed or avoided? My friend Packer says, "You have to play sick to get well." But there is something in this pain that feels overwhelming.

I was telling Ken about that today. How discombobulated I have felt. Out of sorts. That the smallest thing feels overwhelming. For the first time in my life everything feels undone. The irony or sadness of that is that my life was far more undone before than it is now. But in my previous "undoneness" I was so good at holding it all together. But now, sister ain't got one iota of ability to hold up the Titanic. It's pulling me under.

I go to my parents because I'm desperate to be with people. As soon as I get there, I'm desperate to get back home. I need privacy for my grief. It's so crazy. There are moments when you are frantic for a human. To just sit in the room. Watch the television with you. But there are other times when you are desperate to get by yourself, throw yourself on the floor and be the mess that you feel like you are.

Somewhere in the back of my mind it's like I thought, *Once the divorce is final there will be no more crying.* But there is still so much crying. Because there is so much pain to process. Each event, each new first, has some piece of him still attached, until I can make a new memory, which I'm trying desperately to do.

"I just feel out of sorts," I told Ken. "When it starts getting dark outside I don't know what I'm supposed to do."

I could see the compassion on his face. "It takes a great deal of energy to grieve. Because it takes a great deal of energy to heal."

As soon as he said that I got a visual in my head of this wound in my body and everything inside of me rushing to the place of that wound to bring healing to it. And that was when it all made sense. My entire being has rushed to the soul of me, to heal this gaping wound, and it has left me nothing for anything else. It has forced me to change my pace in order to allow my wound to recover. So, all of these frantic and convoluted feelings are normal. In fact, they are healing.

"You need to bring some beauty into your life, Denise."

"I don't know what that means."

"Do things that have beauty in them. That stir up your creativity. Go to the library. Go to the museum. Go to a concert. Go dancing. Those are the things you need to do to replenish your energy. And in doing that it will revitalize your creativity."

I have always pushed myself to produce. So, slowing down to heal is hard for me. Stopping what I'm "supposed" to be doing for what my soul "needs" is not easy. It feels selfish. But, Lord, You have created me this way. You have created a body that will run to the place that needs healing. And for that to become whole, other things may not be as they once were for a season. But what the healing will produce is far more valuable than what the season of healing has forfeited.

I have got to heal. And You know what that is going to take. Help me to surround myself with those things that are beautiful. Breathe life into the soul of me and heal the wounded core of my being.

Day 29

Deneen's request was a simple one. "Do you want to go to Sunday School with us?" It was what came after the request that got me. She began to name all of the couples I knew who were in her class. And she named them as I sat between her and Mark, and my other friends Kim and Lee. But it was another reminder. Another reminder of how my life had changed. Another reminder that I was no longer a couple. I was just a one.

The wailing was like a siren that bounced around my car as I drove home. My anger roared to life right behind it. I ached so much at this life I didn't want. I wanted the sixtieth wedding anniversary. I wanted the wedding ring that would have to be cut off to get it removed. I wanted the grandkids coming by when I no longer had my own teeth and my boobs could be knotted around my neck. And then You allowed me to remember how I got here. Reminding me that sometimes remembering can be your friend, because it prevents you from creating some false reality.

And then I began to pray for the women I knew who had just lost their husbands through death and divorce. And I wept for them. For their loneliness. For their pain. For the fact that they now felt as if they were half of something . . . helping me once again to remember that I'm not the only one I know who is hurting and, for a moment, to forget my own pain. Thank You, Lord, for the ability to remember. Because in remembering I'm learning I can forget.

Day 30

I'm looking at all of the stuff on the counter: the pen, the pencil, the hair clip, the stamps. Each of them has a place. They've always had a place. The pen and pencil go in the drawer by the refrigerator. The stamps go in my office, and the hair clip goes in my bathroom. But at this moment I don't give a rat's rear end about putting them there. By eight o'clock each night my body shuts down. It has given all it can give. And I'm thinking it's a miracle that I can put my pjs on.

You know, it's funny. This morning, after the deep grief of last night, a thought just swept through my mind and I began to thank You. I said out loud, "Thank You, Lord, that someone is coming one day to fulfill desires in me that I have had for years." That's the first time I've done that. That's the first time that I can remember thanking You for what I know You are going to bring.

And even though there are times at night, lying in bed alone, thinking I will die, You are still so present, reminding me that I'm not going to die. I am going to live. And I'm not just going to live, but I am also going to declare how amazing You have been on this journey. How present You have been during this horrific season.

Thank You that the grief of last night has subsided. Thank You that the stuff on the counter can hang out until tomorrow. Thank You that You are meeting every need I have and *will supply all of my needs according to Your riches in Christ Jesus* (see Phil. 4:19). And thank You that You have given me *an anointing that will destroy the works of the devil, and that is my heritage as a servant of the Lord* (see Isa. 54:17).

A friend and I were talking tonight about how we have no idea what we would do without You. I'd be a drug addict for sure. The way I'm addicted to Coca-Cola, it's no doubt. I'm thinking it's much better this way.

Questions

For many people who suffer loss, the feeling of belonging is quickly shattered. Even familiar places can seem foreign or uncomfortable. But you do belong. Take some time to write down all of the people to whom you belong. Next to each name, write down what value you offer these relationships and what value they offer you. In realizing what value we afford to others and they afford to us, we can then make sure that we stay connected, even when our pain would try to cause us to avoid them.

Where can you clearly see that you have shut down your heart? Maybe these are dreams you let go of, talents you laid to the side, things you enjoyed doing but no longer do. As you identify them, begin to pray that God would restore them to you. Joel 2:25 says, "I will restore or replace for you the years that the locust has eaten" (*AMP*).

Behind every action is a motive. It's just the way life works. But very often our motivators can become tainted, skewed and unhealthy. What have been your motivators over the last month for decisions you have made in relationships you are in? What were you looking for? What did you expect to gain? In what ways did it become about you? This question will begin to reveal so much about any unhealthy patterns of behavior. As you begin to identify what the motivators are behind your responses, you can begin to target the mindset that needs to change and the places in your heart that need to be restored.

What are some of the things God has whispered to you over this last month? If you're not hearing Him, begin to pray that your pain will not let you miss Him.

Homework

God doesn't forget our desires. He responds not only to our places of need but also to our desires. What are some of your most-secret desires? Secret things that you've never told anyone. Write them out so that you can be aware of them.

For many of you reading this, you quit doing things you loved years ago. Some of us quit so long ago we might not even remember things that we enjoyed. Let this be a season of rediscovery. Rediscover old things you used to do, and go out and do them again. Join a book club, ride a roller coaster, take dancing lessons, go to the movies all by yourself . . . and begin to discover new things that bring your heart alive. This month spend some time rediscovering old things and discovering new things that bring your heart alive!

Prayer

Lord Jesus, stay with us, for the evening is at hand and the day is past; be our companion in the way, kindle our hearts, and awaken hope, that we may know thee as thou art revealed in Scripture and the breaking of bread. Grant this for the sake of thy love. Amen.

THE BOOK OF COMMON PRAYER

Notes
 1. A. J. Russell, *God Calling Journal* (Ulrichsville, OH: Barbour Publishing, 1996).
 2. Ibid.
 3. Ibid.

MONTH 2

LEARNING TO BE ALONE

(SEPTEMBER)

Day 34

I had three really good days. But today I had to go downtown. I was at the Tennessee Performing Arts Center, a place that held some sweet memories for us a few years back. And opening up that memory bank was as powerful as a crack in a dam. The entire trip home seemed to be laced with memories, and they were refusing to go unnoticed. Hotels held memories, restaurants held memories, roads held memories. And the trip home held nothing but tears and an overwhelming lack of place. I have to stay here in this city packed with our memories. And then I realized that we have memories everywhere—Vegas, Hawaii, Florida, Atlanta, Indiana, California. We have memories in Israel and England and Austria . . . we have memories everywhere. I need new memories, Father. I desperately need new ones. Let this year be a year of making new memories so that I can drive down these streets and not have old memories be my first thoughts. Tonight is a new memory. Tonight I went to TPAC, and it wasn't with him. It was with a friend, my friend . . . my memory. The car ride home . . . our memory. Becoming divorced . . . another piece . . .

Day 37

I'm still struggling with the whole "ex" thing. To actually look at someone and say "my ex-husband," well, I hate it. Surely after all these years and this PC society we would have come up with something better than that. Of course, I'm usually so behind the eight ball, they probably have and I've just never heard of it.

But this is where the journey has me. And yet, as much as I was known, there were so many places I wasn't. Cyndi and I walked out of the theater after watching a romantic comedy, and she looked at me and said, "Do you ever wonder if someone will love you that intensely?" I had an answer, because I had talked about this one day with Ken and come to a revelation even while I was talking. I said, "I have to believe there will be. If I'm able to do that, I have to know that someone else is just as able."

I am grateful, though. Grateful for where my heart is and where my heart is not. I am in a good place. I left my house the other morning, smiling. I decided I needed to find something that would get me out of the house more. So, since I used to substitute teach and really enjoyed it, I decided to apply again. On Friday, I had my first day back to school, and I was so excited. And then I got in the car and immediately thanked You for the opportunity. I found it such a blessing to be able to make money. My own money.

But I know You will provide for everything I need, and all I have to do is trust You to accomplish everything that needs to be accomplished in my life. I thank You, Lord, for Your grace in this season. I thank You that one day someone will put up with even my quirks. Knowing that is a good thing. And knowing for now that it is You and You alone is an even better thing.

Day 38

Well, today I had to tell someone that I was divorced. Before I even started speaking, the tears were brimming on the edge of my lashes and the lump had successfully lodged itself in my throat. The insurance guy asked me something about being married and I said, "He was the man I was married to." It completely allowed me to circumvent having to say that I am divorced. I don't know when it will be okay. But today it isn't, and I'm learning that it's okay if things aren't okay. I am giving myself the freedom for that to be a truth in my life.

I'm also doing things that feed my creativity. The other night I had some of my single friends over and cooked them one more Southern feast. I love to cook. Well, more than that I love to eat my cooking. And I have missed that. I have missed evening dinners and Southern food. I've missed fried chicken and homemade biscuits. I realized that is part of beauty to me. And so, I have been inviting my single friends, widowed friends, divorced friends over and feeding them. And in return we are all being fed. Then we watched *Madea's Family Reunion,* laughed from our toes, took a walk and found pleasure in the entire evening. Three of my favorite things: friends, food and a good movie. Simple things bring me pleasure.

As we were walking tonight, I realized that I miss the walks we used to take after dinner. And it makes me wonder if I'll find someone who enjoys walks, enjoys me, enjoys Madea and enjoys my cooking. And every time those thoughts rush over me I get a burning in my chest. A burning that reminds me that I wanted to still be sitting on the porch with my husband in 40 years, talking about our memories. We would be about 80 but could still have had a lot of life left in us, talking about our grandchildren. We would have been married for more than 50 years and had so much to remember.

I hate that the most. Knowing that I won't have him here to reminisce with me. These were our memories. These were *our* moments. These were our pictures that I'm going to have to pack away, and there is a part of me that wants to, because somehow still having them up makes it seem as if maybe this isn't real. Even this morning I was wondering if maybe my house hadn't sold because he was coming home. But I know I have to move on; it's hard though when you still don't even want to say "my ex-husband."

But You have given me such wonderful blessings. Like the other day, when I went out on the lake with Mark and Deneen. I just wrapped myself up, and as we glided across that sea of glass I just let my soul absorb all of the beauty that surrounded us. What a terrible road filled with immeasurable kindness. Kindness that reminds me that You are in control of every part of this journey.

Even the parts I don't understand. Even the parts that are for my good yet still don't completely quiet the ache in my soul. The beauty comes through my eyes, but it is yet to fill the deepest place of my pain.

I've been reading Philip Yancey's book on prayer, and it makes me wonder if I have treated You flippantly. I don't mean in my heart. I have no desire to see You as a Santa Claus. But do I truly access all of You? I know I don't. But I'm desperate to learn how to know more.

But even the clarity of Your voice in this season has been so affirming. Like yesterday, when I sat in front of the blank computer screen, wondering what would I ever put on it, and You whispered, "If you show up, I'll show up." And You did. Beautifully. Even though it doesn't feel like I'm accomplishing much, You are definitely showing up, so I will too.

I am looking forward to the day though, and I'll thank You for it in advance, when this heaviness lifts from me and I can rest in a real joy of this journey. Granted, I'm always excited knowing that You are with me and have a future for me. And maybe "joy" isn't even the right word, because even in the middle of this pain I have felt Your joy. Maybe what I'm looking for is a complete removal of the grief, the weight and the heaviness. Or maybe it is best if it isn't completely removed. Maybe it's best if it always stays in some measure to remind me of how much I need You. Pain has a way of doing that, you know . . .

Tonight was really challenging. The days sometimes feel so long, and this one has felt eternal. I was sitting in front of the television and was thinking about how long the day had been and then realized it is because my husband would take up so much of my days. I took care of so many of the facets of our business, and I would go to our store two or three times a week, and it just occupied so much of my time; and now it isn't there. So I spend so much of the day wondering what to do with myself. And because my body and spirit and mind are still healing, I have so little energy to do other productive things that I might normally be able to do.

And then last night I went out to a fashion show. It still feels so weird to go out where I know people will see me without my wedding band. I still feel so exposed. So unprotected. Even though You have told me that You've got me. I just still feel like turning my head whenever a man looks my way. They either think I'm the biggest snob in the room or socially dysfunctional, because I still have to figure out who I am in this new world. Where I fit in all of it. I know some semblance of normal will arrive at some point, but I'm just grateful that there are bits of revelation every day.

Day 41

Who's going to eat my broccoli? I sat there staring at my plate tonight at the Japanese steak house, and my broccoli just stared back. He would always tell the chef, before the chef even headed to my plate with broccoli, "You can just give me her broccoli." But tonight, staring at my plate, there was no one to eat it. So I just ate every blasted piece of it myself. I am determined that I will learn to eat it myself, even if I throw up doing it, and I will never have to depend on someone to save me from anything else again. And I know that with that statement lies a huge danger for my heart—the potential to put up a barrier that no one will ever be able to penetrate this shell again. But tonight I was bound and determined that all broccoli eating was going to be done by me.

How did I get here? How did I get to the place where I'm looking at houses by myself? Taking care of my life all by myself? Planning a new life without a man that I love and who stood at the end of an aisle and promised to love me and cherish me and protect me. And now here I am taking care of myself. *I'm* taking care of me. *I'm* planning a life without him, and I just want to know how I got here.

I'm tired tonight. I'm frustrated. I'm angry. All I ever wanted, from the time I was a little girl, was to be loved and cared for and treasured, not left with a plate of broccoli! Did I tell you I hate broccoli?!

And it's not just about the broccoli. It's about the fact that there is comfort in the familiar. I know what he likes to eat. He knows how I like my steak cooked and my favorite restaurant. He knows how I like to be held at night when I go to sleep. I hate this! I hate every part of it! I hate going to bed alone. You know what, maybe I'll start sleeping upstairs in the twin beds. Maybe that won't make it feel quite as painful. Who knows? It just hurts . . . it all hurts . . .

But I have seen You. I promise I've seen You. That is the only piece that gets me through. Help me to see You in everything and to be grateful for everything, even this pain. Tonight I don't know how that is possible, but You know. And today I'm asking for the gift of rest. I'm so tired of crying . . . I'm so tired of hurting . . . I'm so tired . . .

I hear You speaking to me, Father. I hear it right now . . . in my heart. "I give my beloved rest."

I need that tonight, Lord. Rest. No dreaming. No anything. Just rest.

Day 43

I told Ken about the broccoli today. It concerned him . . . my controlled part. The fact that I ate the broccoli instead of just being content with the fact that I don't like it and grieving over the fact that no one would be there to eat it. It made a lot of sense. And I know it's true. He challenged me to really let myself grieve the places that I need to. And I think I did. I think that writing out my pain when I got home had me grieving it. Maybe not in that moment, there at the dinner table, with half of my dinner companions strangers, but I grieved it.

"You might need to pray as well, because there might be some stubbornness in you," Ken said.

I laughed. "You think?"

I'm full of it. I know that. Yet I have always desired to yield my heart to You.

Ken encouraged me to start thinking about myself. Stubbornness I can do, thinking about myself, not so much. I haven't done it in so long that I'm afraid if I start I'll be back on the sofa for my narcissism. I have to laugh at that, but it's true. I have spent the last 15 years making most of life nothing about me. I don't even know how to do it now with my money. I don't know how to spend money on me. So, today I need You to help me learn this. I need to learn how to let what my true heart feels and needs be okay. If I don't like broccoli, I don't have to force it down my throat for the sake of proving a point. I can just push it to the other side. Let it know how utterly despised it is and be perfectly satisfied with the fact that I don't have to eat it. That alone would be thinking about myself. Be careful, Lord . . . if we get me going, I'm not sure where this train might stop.

Day 44

I met with Ken today, and he encouraged me to allow You to be present in those moments when I feel alone. Loneliness stalks me some days. Stays on my heels like my puppy Sophie. And so many times I want to run from that as hard and as fast as I can. So, I distract myself. At home I may turn on the television, watch a show or listen to a sermon. Or maybe that's why I turn on talk radio as soon as I get in the car.

Silence still takes me to places I don't want to travel. It reminds me of how alone I am. How quiet my house is. How lonely my car is. I've had to travel the waters of grief enough inside my marriage and I think that is why I'm running now. But he encouraged me to let You feel present in every situation. To enjoy You and what You bring to my senses and what You want to say to me in those situations.

I need to learn to invite You into my lonely moments and allow for the silence. So I invite You into this moment right now.

I'm lonely. Hurting. But I thank You too. I thank You that I'm not drowning in grief, but surviving through it. And I'm seeing light. I honestly feel like I've caught one tiny hint of light.

Day 45

He and I had to talk today about the yard. About planting new flowers this weekend. Because until the house sells, this is our process. And in our conversation there was a shift. I was asked my opinion. And I didn't give it. Can you believe that? I didn't give it. I could no longer have answers. I know that it was only flowers, but it is time for both of us to discover our own answers, and there seemed no better place to start. Letting go is a process, Father. Being divorced is a process. Today I allowed myself to move one step farther down my path of healing. I didn't give an answer. I didn't have an opinion. I wish I had done that sooner . . .

I was so good at pastoring my husband. I was so good at thinking that I needed to have all of the answers, forgetting what I have come to learn, that to not have all the answers is freeing for everyone. Wish I would have learned that sooner. But my pride kept me from it. My need to rescue kept me from it. My desire to not hurt kept me from it. And in my desperate attempt at self-protection so much was lost.

Father, where would we be if I had quit trying to rescue him? If I had quit trying to play Your role in my husband's life? If I had let failure come years before and the matted mess of our lives unravel however You saw fit? If there is anything that needs to be broken out of me it is this. I'm sure there is a boatload of other things, but this is vital. I cannot rescue; I can shepherd, I can partner, I can encourage. But I cannot rescue. Because in rescuing, I might be standing in the way of someone's healing, of someone's actual encounter with You. Father, forgive me. Forgive me for playing Your role. How arrogant I have been! How aware am I now . . .

Day 48

There was a concert on the lawn tonight. It's one of my favorite things. One of the things that speaks beauty to my heart. Families from our neighborhood gather with their lawn chairs, their children, their drink of choice, and we catch up on the week and listen to some great band play everything from jazz to eighties music. (I love eighties music!) But tonight as I sat there with Cyndi there was a deep sadness. As the children danced around and the parents held each other, watching their little ones in their sweet delight, I leaned over to her and asked, "Will we ever have a normal moment again?" Because in that moment it felt like nothing in my life will ever be normal again. Even though my heart knows it will. There are those moments when it doesn't feel like it will ever be possible again.

So when she left and I could get into the house alone, I only got as far as the floor in the foyer. All I could think was that I was going to have to spend the week by myself. And the saturating awareness of aloneness left me quaking. I couldn't breathe because the heaving rolled in waves that left me spent. I wanted my mom. I just wanted my mom. She had told me in the beginning that if I ever needed her to call her. And I knew I couldn't make this next week by myself. So, I called her. And she's coming.

There are moments in this journey when You are enough. There are moments when I feel You covering me, holding me and loving me. And then there are moments when I need that love to come to me through real arms, audible words and a human touch. And in those moments I have found You just as present and just as healing. I don't think it is weakness; I choose to see it as humanness. Humanness that You made and that You love. But even if it is weakness, the beauty is that right smack dab in the middle of it, I'm going to find Your strength.

Day 50

Today Mom and I went back to my home church. For almost the past four months I have been attending my brother's church.

This morning when I walked through the doors it felt like home. But then tonight, I had this feeling that if I returned there I would be missing something. I have felt a real need to remove myself from the comfortable. To branch out. Yet the other church still doesn't feel like me. My home church seems to fit me and my style of worship. Yet my heart feels a tug toward my brother's church. So this is another place where I am yet called to trust You. There has been a lot of letting go lately. To think of letting go, of risking one more thing, makes me weary. To think of missing You makes me willing to risk anything.

I see things so differently now. Divorce does that. It changes the very lens from which you view life. Ironically, what is more settled in me is how easily marriage can work. When out-serving one another is the goal, few things seem to be as big a deal. It really comes down to the simple way You've called us to love. So this past week I was listening to a friend of mine who hasn't been married long and is dealing with some foundational questions of his own life. But his question to me was, "What has kept you so close to God?" The question caused me to try to figure it out. Because the way he asked it led me to believe that he thinks I have something that isn't available to everyone. As if I've cornered the market on You. As if You respond to me differently than You respond to anyone else.

There have even been moments in this journey when I've felt guilty for how sweetly You have loved me and moved on my behalf. But when I remember that I have been buried for so long, as if being fertilized, I realize that this is simply a season of all that was percolating underground finally coming to the surface. I didn't wake up today and find You moving this way. I have been pressing hard into You for years, desperate for You because of the pain of where I was. What has kept me close? I have simply surmised that I have never retreated. Even in those seasons when Your silence was deafening and in those seasons when I couldn't understand what seemed like Your lack of movement, when all I wanted to do was run, I stayed. I'm not perfect. I'm just stubborn . . .

Day 54

Some of the girls and I saw the new Tyler Perry movie last night. I loved every minute of it. I just enjoyed living last night. I soaked every piece of it up. The laughter from the audience, the images on the screen, the music that filled the movie theater, the way some of the audience talked back, the taste of the popcorn and Coke. It was beautiful and real.

Day 58

We're having a baby! Well, not me, but Damon and Sarah! I can't believe it. Well, I can . . . I knew they wanted one, but it just feels like a burst of life during a season of death. They were so excited. I was the first person they told. They were petrified I wasn't going to be home, because I had gone out for a little while. Since Mom had left, I didn't want to be here alone. But what wonderful news to get tonight! And the excitement of being able to be here and experience all of this with them! Thank You, Lord, for this sweet and beautiful gift . . .

And look at the date too. Four days since my last entry! Every time I have days in between journal entries like this I feel as if I'm healing. Each day brings a sense of healing in some way though because it moves me a little farther from where I was the day before. And tonight, knowing that life is coming . . . well, that's just another little piece.

Day 61

Since the day I got married we were both home together. There was always life in the house except during the times when he was on the road. And in these final years, especially the ones when his business was in our house, there was such activity. And now, I can go entire days and see no one if I choose to. But I can't. I have to have people. Even if that means going back to substitute teaching or doing my work over at the pool where I can at least hear people laugh. So this week my goal was to have dinner with someone.

Tuesday night Ronda and I went out to dinner. And Wednesday I went out with Tina. I'm just desperate to be with people I know and who know me. Being in the places where I am known is so important for me right now when it feels like there are so many places I'm not known.

I'm also having to learn the difference between healthy distractions and simply distracting myself from my pain. I am confronting the loneliness. The other side of the bed still holds an element of coldness, even though I have gone to sleeping in the middle of it. Most of my dinners are in front of the television now, but we had gotten to that point anyway. And I'm learning that talking out loud to You and engaging You in conversation is really enjoyable. You're enjoyable, do You know that? Crazy, I know. You know everything. But I enjoy You . . . and if You'll hang in there with me, I'm confident this is going to turn into a beautiful mess. I can only describe this as "wonderful as horrible can be."

Day 62

Packer and I left for the Joy Spring retreat today. Few ministries hold a place in my heart like this place. I'll never forget going 11 years ago at the most broken place in my life separate from this one. I'm not sure what a nervous breakdown looks like, but if I did, I'm certain I was as close to having one as a person could get. And there in the middle of my brokenness, in a cabin overlooking the hills of Tennessee, You whispered so beautifully to me: "I have brought you here to restore your joy." And You did. You did something supernatural in me that weekend that I honestly believe gave me the ability to survive these past 11 years. I have never forgotten that moment. And it has kept my heart connected to this ministry, and the joy of watching what it does in the lives of others.

Packer and I met everyone at Cracker Barrel for dinner, and we were seated with this precious couple from Alabama. As they began to share their story with us, they told us of their daughter's death from cancer a few years back. The father looked at me and said, "It is a scientific fact that holding on to offenses feeds cancer. And my daughter was incapable of forgiving anyone."

I began to immediately think of this journey—the bitterness, the anger, the pain that can saturate you. Yet, in Your mercy, You have given me the ability to let it go. It caused me to think of someone I knew who had died from cancer a couple years back that had been incapable of forgiving as well. Every bad thing ever done to them they had chronicled as if on index cards to pull out and recount whenever anyone would listen. Holding on to their gaping wound like a sign of their martyrdom. Living in the bondage that bitterness brings.

All I know to do in this moment is thank You. With the journey I've walked, bitterness would be so easy to grab hold of and not let go. But somehow, in Your mercy, You have given me the strength to let go. The gift is that I've wanted to. And I know that is key in healing. I couldn't have done it with You.

Day 63

I received a powerful word from You today through our speaker Paul Godava. He spoke over me that in one day all of my heavy grief would be gone. That it would be like the prayers that are being prayed for me would accumulate as heat in a hot air balloon and would lift the grief that I was under in one moment. And that the miracles that followed would leave me saying, "This is too good to be true." I left with expectation . . . beautiful expectation.

Day 65

Packer and I got lost today. Hopelessly, hysterically lost. I hate mountains. I am a "shortest distance between two points is

a straight line" kind of girl. As we were leaving the Joy Springs retreat, I told the men who gave us directions, "Please, if this is
longer, I'd just as soon get to the interstate." But nnoooooooooo . . .
they knew exactly where we needed to go. "It's just over the mountain," they said. Four hours later, two of those spent going down
the wrong road and putting us back in Tennessee when we were
headed to Atlanta, finally had us traveling through Helen, Georgia, which I have since otherwise renamed. You can figure out
what I'm calling it now.

All I wanted was to get to Atlanta, go to Buckhead Diner, and
go see a movie. I had our night planned before my SIBA (Southern Independent Booksellers Alliance) event tomorrow. And that
got blown to smithereens! I mean, by the time we got to Helen,
Georgia, after we had driven through almost every small town in
Tennessee that looked like it could vie for a scene out of *Deliverance*, we made it to Helen just in time for their parade. People were
all over the streets with their beer steins, German music blared
from the restaurants and the Elvis impersonator in his Cadillac
convertible waved to us as he passed by. That was when we lost it.
I mean tears-rolling-down-our-faces laughing.

Packer made this statement at one point, "Denise, there are
destination people and there are journey people. I'm thinking you
are a destination person." I said, "You think?"

But I'm learning. I enjoyed the journey enough to laugh in
the middle of the mayhem, stop and get a Coke (of which she ru-
ined hers by putting salted nuts into it) and finally get to Atlanta
without being angry over the fact that we didn't have time for a
movie. Over our dinner at Buckhead Diner we started cracking
up all over again and I felt the laughter in my toes . . . I felt it all
the way in my toes.

Thank You, Lord, that in the middle of grief I can laugh. A
belly laugh. Help me learn more how to enjoy the journey. I've
missed so much of life simply trying to survive. I don't think it's
that I hate the journey piece. I think it's hard to experience it
when your soul is dead. I'm becoming alive, Father. Thank You
that today, on this journey, I was exceptionally alive.

Questions

There are often things that you enjoyed doing when you were married that you think have to stop once you're divorced. For me it was cooking dinner. The pain was that I love my own cooking.☺ What are some of the things you have stopped doing that you really enjoyed doing when you were married? What are some things you can do to get those pleasures back into your everyday life again?

Have you had broccoli moments? You know, moments when you have determined you were going to do something simply because you were not going to depend on anyone else to do it for you? What do you see as the danger in this way of thinking? What is something that you need to give yourself permission simply to not do?

Grief can feel selfish. Yet, it requires so much of us. So, to think that there should be a season that's just about you, especially if you have given to others to an unhealthy degree, is very hard to do. Yet grief needs you. It needs you to be present in order to heal. What are some ways you need to start making life more about you, even if you run the risk of being selfish?

Loneliness in this season can seem to stalk you. But it won't kill you. You might actually discover that God is very present in it. How can you invite Him into your loneliness the next time you are in the middle of that place of pain? I encourage you to do it.

Homework

Invite some friends to do something with you that you and your spouse used to do. Maybe it is cooking a big dinner, going to a movie, going to your favorite restaurant. Reclaim something that was yours. Just because your spouse is gone doesn't mean you can't do it anymore.

Go someplace alone that you and your spouse loved to go. Invite God into that entire experience with you. Talk to Him through it. Tell Him what you're feeling. Ask Him what He desires to speak to you about it. And enjoy His presence in that moment. Cry if you need to. Journal if you want to. But run into it, not from it.

Prayer

O God of peace, who hast taught us that in returning and rest we shall be saved, in quietness and confidence shall be our strength: By the might of thy Spirit lift us, we pray thee, to thy presence, where we may be still and know that thou art God; through Jesus Christ our Lord. Amen.

THE BOOK OF COMMON PRAYER

MONTH 3

LETTING GO

(OCTOBER)

Day 67

I cried this morning as he and I talked. And there has been this heaviness resting on the top of my heart all day. Probably because that is where love resides. And the pressure seems to stay there mostly. I'm sad. And it's so hard to understand all that I feel. He kept the girls for me while I was on my trip, and I had to go last night and pick them up. When I saw him it felt so strangely unfamiliar, yet there was still this sense of familiarity at the same time. I mean, one day you walk into "your" store and the next day you walk into "your ex-husband's" store, and nothing looks like yours, and yet you know it as if it's still yours. You know the way it feels, the way it sounds, the way it moves and the way it is.

Even when I look at him he is strangely not mine. Yet still mine. And in my heart I miss talking to him. I miss spending the evenings with him. And yet there is so much I don't miss. So much that swallowed me whole and all but sucked the life out of me; and now that I am experiencing living, I see him differently. I've watched so often when people lose a spouse—to death especially—how all of sudden that spouse almost begins to get immortalized. I don't want to do that here, Father. We didn't get to this place because of how healthy we were. We got here because of our extreme brokenness. And I need to remember that. Because remembering that will prevent me from making this something it wasn't and, in return, slowing my own personal healing.

But do You know what is familiar in all this? You . . . I can feel how You treasure me. And I have hope too. Hope for a future. Hope for the calling on my life. Hope of something more than what I've known. Today I was listening to Bible teacher Joyce

Meyer, and she was talking about faithfulness. Your faithfulness. She read from Isaiah 61:7: "Instead of your shame you will have a double portion" (*NASB*). That is all I know to ask for, Lord. That somehow this intense place of shame this new life has generated will be replaced with a double portion.

In fact, I am taking this as my own. I am going to believe that You have a double portion for me. Double the love . . . double the dreams . . . double the provision . . . double the divine appointments . . . double the anointing . . . double the revelations . . . double the wisdom . . . double the discernment. All these things, Lord, are what I am going to be praying and believing for. And they also are what I know You have for me.

I thank You that You are here in the middle of this difficult season and You are working mightily to save me . . . "Instead of humiliation they will shout for joy over their portion. Therefore they will possess a double portion in their land, everlasting joy will be theirs" (Isa. 61:7, *NASB*).

Day 68

Am I angry? I had my counseling appointment today and I shared with Ken a conversation I had two days ago with my former husband when I picked up my dogs. Then I had a horrible dream last night, and in it I had this huge outburst of anger, and so I asked Ken, "Do you think I'm angry?"

He said, "I'm sure you are. After 13 years, I'm sure you haven't dealt with all your anger."

"But I don't feel angry. Like right now. I don't feel angry." I paused. "I don't think I'm angry."

He was pretty gentle with me. "Why don't you ask the Lord if there is any anger in there that He wants you to deal with?"

"Okay, but I'm pretty sure I'm not angry."

He smiled and nodded.

Maybe I am angry. Maybe I've hidden so much of my true anger through the years because of fear. Fear of how others would

Anger is essential to healing

respond to it. Fear of what the consequences of it would be. Fear of the pain or confrontation that anger can bring about. And yet, I know that You aren't the author of fear. And I know that anger can be a healthy response to things that are simply wrong. And I know that it is essential to healing.

Ken wanted me to go back and list 50 things that I'm angry about. I can't imagine being angry about 50 things. Who knows how many I can actually list. I doubt there are any at all.

He also encouraged me to look for that chasm between my passions and where I am. And I realized that I am having to learn what it is that I actually enjoy. What I want and don't want to do for my life. What I'm truly passionate about. For so long I haven't even known what I was passionate about because I allowed myself to become swallowed whole by someone else. And in the middle of that so much of what You placed in me was shut down.

But I'm learning. Like the other day when I went out and bought some necklaces for no other reason than that they made me feel pretty. I also bought a dress that I probably wouldn't have bought a year ago, and I love it! So, I'm learning. I'm learning that You made me intensely passionate. There are places where I can see it. I see it in the stories You have been so gracious to let me write. And I feel it in my deep place whenever I get to teach. But I am having to learn about what passion looks like in my everyday life. Just in living. And this week I tapped into it. And my necklace looks dang good! Becoming divorced . . . just another piece of the journey.

Day 70

Okay. I'm angry. Know it without a doubt. And it all came to life tonight over a jar of sweet potato butter. I picked up the jar so I could slather it on a biscuit. And I couldn't open it. It didn't matter what I did. I pounded it with a knife. Ran it under hot water. And with each twist, with each pull, with each pounding, I got angry. By the time the water had scalded my fingers the tears had scalded my face and the anger had scalded my soul. The self-control that prevented me from throwing the jar across the room with a guttural scream, well, I'm still not sure where that came from. So I slammed the jar down on the counter, not caring if it splattered in a thousand little pieces and left remnants of sweet potato butter on everything from my hair to the back door. I went straight to my computer and began to type out my anger.

I was like Madea on her calculator, from *Diary of a Mad Black Woman*. And before I had taken a deep breath I had 50 things I was angry about. And I wept through all of them. The heaving was relentless. With the tapping of every key the revelation of my anger became more and more apparent. But do You know what is so crazy about it all? After I typed out all of the things that make me angry I didn't stop there. I made a new line. I began to type out things that I had appreciated about him over these last five months. My words held the extremes of David's emotions in the psalms. Yet it was the only way I knew to do it. I couldn't just be angry. I had to caveat my anger with my gratitude.

Lord, that could be the most dysfunctional piece about me, or the most beautiful part of me. I think I'll choose to believe the latter. But there again, "choosing to believe the best" got me to the divorce courts. Yet, "choosing to believe the best" in You has gotten me through.

❋   ❋   ❋

When I finally crawled into bed I was spent. You would think my mind wouldn't have had the strength to travel anywhere else. Yet it found some places, probably unearthed by my anger. And lying there in the dark I began to have this fear of allowing anyone to ever touch me again intimately. What would that be like? When I had at one time allowed someone to know me so well, how could I ever let anyone else know me that way again?

And the pain of that feels so real. Even though it has been so long. So, here I am—bringing to You this most intimate place. Telling You clearly that I can't imagine it. Don't want it. Dread it.

Fear it . . . and somewhere in the middle of all of that, You merci-
fully let me go to sleep.

Day 73

There is still work to do. I still wake up to responsibility. Yet
writing hasn't even been on my radar since I wrote those six pages.
My new book is launching this month, and for the life of me I
don't know what my next book will be. I have ideas. I always have
ideas. But there is no thought connecting to words connecting to
paper. There is just a clutter of ideas and a gratefulness that no
book I've ever written, to this point, has been done by me. Good
thing, huh. Because if You hadn't shown up as I've written each
one, there would be a lot of white space.

But today I am in the middle of contract negotiations. My
publisher has offered me a new three-book deal. In the middle of
all of this uncertainty, that offer feels like something so solid. So
certain. Yet, I am filled with a deep unsettledness. Maybe it is where
I am. Maybe it is the fact that life as I know it has forever changed
and my ability to view this with clarity and real perspective is
skewed by the hole in my soul and the often yuck in my gut. But
somehow this feels different.

My publisher wants an answer. All I have right now are more
questions. And yet in the middle of all the uncertainty of what
should feel certain, You continue to remind me that You are present and that I won't miss You. This feels similar to my decision
about church. So I need to hear from You. Once again . . . I need
to hear from You.

Day 74

Last night I was reading through my devotional from last
year on today's date, and all I can think is, *Man, this year
has sucked. I've lost so much.* But every time I think about what I've

lost, quickly all that You have shown me follows. You have been so present. And the opportunities You've given me have been amazing.

Like where I am today. Books-a-Million has a managers' dinner for all their managers once a year. It is their national conference and they only invite a few authors. And they invited me. Me . . . I listened last night as Jan Karon was one of their keynote speakers and spoke so candidly about You. And I thought, *I'm going to do that one day. One day I'm going to be a bookstore's keynote speaker and I'm going to speak unashamedly about how undeservedly good You are.*

You know what else? Last night when I was getting all dressed up in my hotel room for the dinner, I looked in the mirror. The first feeling that tried to overtake me was my extreme loneliness. I pushed back at it and reminded myself that You were with me. When I walked into the large room and saw the strange faces all around, it pushed hard again. The desire to have a human companion was deep and pressing and real. But I do have a companion, and I am never alone. Thank You for getting me through what could have ended in another really ugly cry, and I already had my makeup on. Thank You for walking with me into every room I enter.

Day 75

Okay, I now know why I felt so bad writing that list of things that made me angry and then had to follow it up with good things too. Because that was the cycle. One moment of good could make it seem as if the bad didn't exist, and I would almost pretend that the tough things had never really happened.

So this is clearly a pattern of behavior. I have to learn that it is okay for things to have their proper emotion. If things make me angry, it's okay to simply be angry. I don't have to find something to appease that, to make that okay. Anger can be a healthy and needed emotion at times. Because bad things still need to be addressed and they still need to be dealt with. If you don't deal with them, then you become the perpetual compartmentalizer and nothing ever gets resolved. Life stands in limbo, hanging in a balance of the imbalanced. The story of my life. Trying to seem balanced when I am the poster child for imbalanced. This was a real revelation to me today. And with it I had the ability to go back and finish the list without feeling guilty for being angry. And even in some of those things that I am angry about—the dreams never fulfilled, the promises never kept—there is a sense of gratitude that many never came to be. Because had they, I'm not sure I would be here right now, experiencing You the way I am, walking in a place of wholeness like I've never known.

I saw him today too. And it's all so very sad. I wonder if I'll always care. Because today it feels as if I'll care forever.

My brother wants to introduce me to someone. He and Sarah have said so much about this guy that I actually dreamed about him last night. I dreamed about having a date with him. And all I can think about is all the ways that I'm afraid someone might want to change me. This guy is in the health industry. So much so that he wrote a book about it! Well, I drink Coke and eat fried chicken. Sure, I've done boot camp for the last two years, but thinking about someone sitting across the table from me and telling me they don't know what Crisco is scares the living daylights out of me, if I'm just being honest. (Of course I'm sure he knows what Crisco is and has 10 reasons why it will kill you. But for the record, my granny cooked with it every day and lived to be 80!)

But all of it just freaks me out. I don't want someone coming in and trying to change everything about me to conform to who he is. Granted I know that relationships require some give and take and compromise. But I just want our whole pieces to fit together . . . well . . . wholly. So, if that can be a prayer, then that is what I'm praying.

Plus, how does your heart make room for someone else when it feels like someone else already resides there? How does someone else ever fit? I guess the heart has to grow. And it does have this amazing ability to continually expand. I mean, I've had Maggie for almost 13 years, and when we got Chloe, my love expanded. Then I grieved so much over her when she died. Even now, when I think of that final evening before she died and that look—that "I'm so tired, Mommy" look—my love for her is still there. That ache still rests inside of me. Yet my heart had the ability to take this little Sophie in, and love simply exploded again. My heart expanded. And even as I'm writing this I realize that is probably what love will look like when it comes to me. Even though the questions remain. How is it that I could have loved my husband for so many years and now be expected for that love to vaporize, never to return, when I know that some piece of my heart will be his for the rest of my life?

That is where I carry him, you know. The heart is so big and so complex and so hard to fathom. It pumps life through me. It beats inside of me. It expands to hold everything that I hold dear; and when one person takes their leave it breaks. As if a piece of it breaks off and leaves with that person. Or as if the person is removed from it and a hole remains that is shaped like them and will leave a perpetual reminder.

I'm not sure my former husband will ever really be gone. Maybe he will. But I'm not sure how. He'll still escape from my memories every now and then. And I'm sure there are places where he will be embedded into my soul. But my heart will expand. The memories we shared will blur. And maybe a new love can melt me. I know I look at my Sophie and she sure has melted me. And maybe like her I'll want a new love to hold me and love me. And just like Sophie he will want that too . . . maybe I'm not as scared as I thought.

Ken and I had a great session today. He wanted me to read the list I had written. My "angry list" I call it. I didn't want to read it. But he pressed me into reading it. So, I was pretty defiant about it. "Okay, but I'm not going to cry."

"Yes you are," he said.

I knew he wasn't joking. But I determined I wasn't going to cry.

I read through the first five without a tear. He stopped me. "Where are you while you're reading this?"

"Completely disconnected," I responded.

"That's what I thought." He sat there and looked at me.

I felt the tension in my shoulders loosen. I extended my wrist, letting the paper fly in front of my face. "If I connect with this I'm going to cry at number three. I know I will. I'll cry at number three." And then I broke down but quickly swiped at my tears and tried to gather myself.

"Why do you pull it back together?"

"Because I don't want to lie on your floor weeping like a baby. I try to do that alone."

He didn't respond to that. But I could tell by his expression that the fact that I at least was made it okay.

Then I changed the subject from my anger to my fears. "I'm afraid of a new relationship, Ken. I'm afraid of what my heart will gravitate toward. I'm afraid that all of the dysfunctional patterns of my own behavior are going to come back to the surface and I'm going to get it all wrong."

He looked at me in that soft way that he does. "Denise, the more whole you become the farther from those actions and decisions you'll get. The more you get in touch with what you're truly passionate about, you're going to move farther away from those things that you gravitated toward."

Something in that statement gave me so much peace. Such deep peace. I think he could see it on my face. Because he laughed.

"I want you to be my client forever."

I laughed. "No way! I don't want to stay here forever."

When we both gathered ourselves this time, I looked at him. "Ken, I want the man I marry to read my books."

He looked at me. "The man who marries you will want to read your books."

My heart agreed. It strongly agreed. "It's the relearning part. I don't want to be relearned."

"You know, my fear is that you are going to build up this big wall around your heart and you might miss a really great person."

"But what if he doesn't like my fried chicken?" I felt the panic rise up quickly. "I know that he likes corn out of a bag, but I like fresh corn from the garden. I know he likes his corn cut off the cob and I like mine on the cob. How do you go through the process of all of that with someone else? It makes me heartsick to think about."

He leaned up closer. "But what if someone likes your chicken just the way it is? And likes your corn, just the way it is?"

I have to admit that made me smile. The thought of that made me smile.

He leaned back and crossed one leg over the other. "Why don't you read a little more?"

He was smart. He had me smiling before he made me go further. But it wasn't number three that got me; it was number five. "For not letting me be able to let my little girl wear my wedding dress." And I crumbled. Completely fell apart.

"You're really going to have to grieve that one, Denise."

My shoulders were shaking from my tears. "I know. It is so painful." He let me sit there with my tears. He's always gracious to do that. Then he finally broke the heaviness.

"What do you hear when someone tells you you're beautiful?"

"Well, he used to tell me that."

"I'm not talking about your outward beauty. That is there, but I'm talking about the whole of you."

I didn't know how to take that in. I didn't know how to take in beauty the way he intended for me to in that moment. The only way I knew to respond was, "Well, I feel like I'm a good person and I believe that there are other good people out there who have to be willing to commit their whole heart to someone."

"I believe that too."

I left the office with the word "beauty" ringing in my ears. Do I truly know what that word means? Father, there is so much buried on the inside of me. So much. Help me dig through it and learn . . . truly learn . . . how You see beauty. And how You see me.

Day 78

I had my book launch party for *The Will of Wisteria* today at Landmark Booksellers. The room was filled with faces of sweet friends, and smiles of strangers. They welcomed my story into their hearts; they laughed when I read from its pages; and when it was all over we took pictures, and for one more moment I forgot. Once again, You so graciously gave me a moment where my heart was fully present, and the pain of where I am was briefly forgotten.

I remember when I was writing that book that it was during such a dark season. It was during the months before I delivered divorce papers. It was during that season when I was carrying so much privately. When I knew where I was headed, but my world had yet to officially change. Yet my soul was breaking up on the inside. That I turned the book in at all is a miracle. And then when I did, I turned it in pretty pitifully. My editor actually scolded me, then apologized for her scolding. I assured her it was deserved. Come to find out, she was walking through almost the exact same grief at the exact same time. Because of our utter dependence on You, I believe this is the best book I've ever written. That, and the fact that she is such a fabulous editor.

So, celebrating this today is a huge achievement . . . a huge acknowledgment of Your grace. And what a sweet day You gave me. My precious friends were there to support me, and then we went to one of my favorite little Japanese joints and then headed to a movie. I'm continually amazed how in the middle of death You still birth things. What a gift this book is to me for this season! What a piece of life in the middle of what is dying.

❋   ❋   ❋

I thought about him intimately tonight. Is that wrong now that we're not married anymore? I guess it is, huh? Unless it is remembering . . .

but I don't think that is what this was. I think this was simply day-dreaming about this man that I have so loved, wondering if I could ever love him intimately again. But I had wondered that for a long time, hadn't I? Divorce happens slowly . . . You said that . . . piece by piece . . . longing by longing . . . memory by memory.

Day 79

On the way to church I had two thoughts. The first one is this huge contradiction of one minute being certain that I never want another man to touch me again and then the next minute wondering about who You may have for my future. There are a couple of specific people I've thought about, but for different reasons I'm praying it won't be them. And then, when I think of the kind of man my heart desires, I immediately disqualify myself by thinking, *I'm not pretty enough for that, or good enough to get a man like that.* I look at my "girls" that have drifted from the heights of my twenties; the lines on my face; my age; and I doubt myself in the area of what I'm even capable of attracting. But then, in Your sweet way, I felt like You let me know that if I would allow You that You want to blow my mind here too. So, I will allow You . . .

My second thought was what it would be like the first time I kiss someone else. The only man I have kissed for 15 years has been him. And I was thinking, *I don't want to go around kissing someone if they're not the one You have for me. I want to kiss just one. The one that You have for me is the only one I want to kiss.* And with the thought soars the anger—the anger that I have to even think about this at all.

As I pulled into a parking place at church this morning the thoughts of kissing were completely curtailed by my rage. When I climbed out of the car there was no one to make sure I looked okay. He used to always check my shirt or coat or jacket before we'd go into church to make sure that after I had brushed my hair and gotten ready for church or wherever I was going that my back was as neat and tidy as my front. That no stray hairs had decided to hang around on my clothes. But he wasn't there to do that today.

So in my anger, I just jerked my coat around until I looked like a contortionist and checked myself. And the whole time I'm turning my jacket around I'm thinking, *Thank You, Lord, that I'm not wearing a dress.* And then, having the brief concern that I might actually be schizophrenic because, my word, I've gone through just about every emotion imaginable today and had them all while talking to myself out loud!

And now I'm back in the place of being reminded of all the things I have to do all by myself. Check my own clothes. Drive myself home. Fix dinner for just me. Watch television alone. All of it. And in the middle of this storm that is raging around me like a category 4, You whisper *peace* . . . but my storm doesn't come to an immediate halt. Maybe it's because I'm slightly more stubborn in letting it go. But as I slowly release my grip, I feel the pace of my heartbeat slow . . . the rage in my gut release and the reality of my life settle into a survivable place.

Day 81

"I'm not going back. I'm moving ahead. I'm here to declare to You the past is over. In You . . . all things are made new. Surrendered my life to Christ. And I'm moving . . . moving forward." Those were the lyrics from my new CD from Free Chapel, coming over the speakers in my rental car today. I left for the first part of my book tour, and while the tires connected with the asphalt, my heart connected with these lyrics, and I am . . . I'm moving forward. I'm not going back to the life that I had. That is evident. And honestly, as deep as the love ran from me to him, it isn't a life that I would ever want to live again. I was so broken.

I spent years not even listening to love songs. I spent years where I had lost the ability to sing—something I had loved to do. Shoot, I hardly listened to music anymore, let alone love songs. Give me talk radio and let me hear someone else's drama. But somewhere in all of this my love for music has returned.

Things are starting to come to life again. And I'm moving forward. I can't believe it . . . I'm moving forward.

Granted I'm not completely forward. If someone asked me to go out with them today I think I'd have to say, "Here's my number, call me in six months. I'm still screwed up!" I'm sure that would be one of the top 10 ways of *how to snag a man in six months or less.* So maybe everything isn't in complete forward motion, but I bet I'd know they were worth it if they actually called back in six months.

But I am moving forward in my healing. I really am. The ache for him is getting farther and farther away. I ache over what we lost. What could have been. But I'm not aching as much over him. I mean, sometimes I do. Like right now, typing this, I can see his face, and I do miss him. And I wish so much he had found us worth fighting for. But there is one thing worth fighting for today, and that is forward momentum. It's started, and I'm not letting it go.

Day 84

Lord, I know people think You don't care about the details. That when people in other countries are dying, You don't care about the tiny, little secret places of our hearts. I used to wonder too. But after the past seven months with You I know that You care about every detail of my heart. And tonight You just took pleasure in delighting me.

You know I'm Southern and believe that fried foods should be their own food group, and that Paula Deen should be the official cook in heaven along with my mama, of course. And it had been a long day. My childhood friend, Joan, who I call sister, and I had come to Savannah for this leg of my book tour, and after my book signing tonight at Barnes and Noble, there was just one place we wanted to go, The Lady and Sons. They said that the reservations were full and that there were no more seatings, but I knew that if you got there close to closing there was the possibility you could find some seats at the bar. Because anyone can sit there if there are open seats. So I dropped Joan off at the door and she called me and told me to park . . . that we could sit at the bar. Well, we were as giddy as schoolgirls.

When we got to the hostess counter the girl led us to a table. Not the bar. To a table! Right there in the middle of the dining room! We almost told her she got it wrong, that we were to be sequestered at the bar. That we were completely comfortable in the "eat your fried chicken at the smoky bar" table because it was, after all, Paula Deen's fried chicken! But we didn't move. We even sat at the table for a few moments staring at our menus, afraid to move, thinking for sure that in a minute the Paula Deen police were going to come snatch us from our chairs and throw us out on the corner. But the only thing that came to the table was the waiter. The waiter! My word, we were about to do the Pentecostal Happy Dance right there. You know the kind where they spin around like a helicopter. If we hadn't been so hungry and knew we wouldn't have passed out from the twirling, I bet we would have given it a whirl.

We ordered sweet tea, because can't nobody make it like Miss Paula, and then we headed to the buffet—a buffet that they were still putting fresh food on even after the last seating had already taken place. We fixed our plates: low country boil, corn on the cob, mac and cheese, homemade cheese biscuits . . . We sat down eating like two pigs in slop! It was the one thing we wanted to do here. Granted, I came to work, but all I could think about was getting some food at Paula Deen's. I know people would think, *You girls sure were lucky.* But, Lord, I simply choose not to see it that way. I sensed You smiling. Whether You stopped the world for us tonight or not, whether it was You who gave us a perfect dinner at one of our favorite restaurants or not, I'm still thanking You.

You say that "every good thing given and every perfect gift is from above" (Jas. 1:17, *NASB*). And tonight, Father, felt like a really good and perfect gift in a rather less than perfect season. So, I'm deciding to thank You for this. A sweet night, Lord. A really sweet night.

Day 85

I'm living in the most uncertain time of my life—a time when my heart desires things to remain as they are. Where peace and comfort rule. Yet today I feel You asking me to do something I never dreamed You would ask me to do. Today You are asking me to walk away from a three-book deal with a company that knows me and respects me, and an editor that I adore. You're asking me to leave certainty for more uncertainty. You're asking me to jump off a cliff from a height that is staggering to a bottom that can't be seen. You're asking me to trust You. Again.

This is crazy! I mean, crazy faith! Crazier still is the peace I feel. No, it's more than that. It's excitement. With every step into nothingness You have asked me to step, and with every landing my foot has safely found, my faith has been built. And so I take this step with excitement. I am genuinely excited. Because I know there is no way You would ask me to do this if there wasn't something even better on the other side of it. Something that I would miss if I stayed in what is comfortable. (How much have I missed by staying in the comfortable?)

Father, what a season we've had. I remember at the close of last year when You gave me Psalm 126: "When the LORD brought back the captives to Zion, we were like men who dreamed. Our mouths were filled with laughter, our tongues with songs of joy. Then it was said among the nations, 'The LORD has done great things for them.' The LORD has done great things for us, and we are filled with joy. Restore our fortunes, O LORD, like streams in the Negev. Those who sow in tears will reap with songs of joy. He who goes out weeping, carrying seed to sow, will return with songs of joy, carrying sheaves with him" (*NIV*).

When I took this as a word from You so directly spoken to my life last year, I thought it meant that You were going to restore my marriage and I would be like one who had dreamed. But that's not what You did. Yet it is all still so true. I feel like someone who is living a dream, who has been released as a captive and who is experiencing You as never before. I'm laughing now. I'm singing again.

And I continue to tell people all the amazing things that You have done for me, yet my eyes are sharpened at the beautiful things You are doing for others. But You also said You would restore the fortunes . . . quickly, like torrents. And, Lord, the things that have transpired over these last seven months You have done so quickly. I may have gone out weeping last year, but I am coming in with joy. And I am bringing the harvest of that pain with me. And part of that is this ability to trust You when it looks crazy . . . foolish even.

Lord, my writer friends are going to think I'm an idiot. This is a contract that many of them would love to have. And yet, I am walking away having no idea of the real reason why, only knowing that You are calling me. And in that I will trust. You are taking me places I sure didn't plan on going this year. I never dreamed I'd lose my Chloe. Never dreamed I'd lose my marriage. Never dreamed I'd walk away from certain work, when financially I need everything that I have. Yet I am doing all of it with peace . . . and joy too! Oh, my word, sister has gone and lost her mind!

You have a plan in all of this, of that I am confident about. So, I'll walk wherever You choose to take us. And thank You for giving me exactly what I needed for my peace. I trust that You have another door. A better door for the purposes of Your plan for my future. And I'm moving forward with expectation. Expectation in You.

Day 86

I'm in Columbia today where I did a book event for the South Carolina Teachers Association as a guest of Books-A-Million. Still enjoying the joy of yesterday and the excitement of my future. That was when he called, angry. In this entire journey there have been few encounters. One of the amazing things about it is the kindness that we have afforded each other.

I knew I would get this call. I knew that when he found out about a certain situation he would be angry. But what I found in this moment was the opportunity to stop an old pattern of behavior—my pattern of behavior that tries to be peacemaker; that piece in me that wants everyone to be happy with me and happy with each other. He hung up on me, and I had to fight so hard against the desire to try to fix everything and make it okay. I almost, for a brief moment, even took up his offense. Another dangerous pattern in me; I simply wanted him to be okay. I didn't want him to hurt.

I went to a place of self-pity momentarily. *How do I always end up in the middle?* But the beautiful part is the moment of collapse that would have normally lasted for a day, a couple days, a week, was just that . . . a moment. You gave me the strength in my weakness, allowing me to fight through giving the enemy my day.

I thought about Myrtle's words to Helen in *Diary of a Mad Black Woman*: "Can't nobody make me happy and can't nobody make me mad." I realized in order for him to take my peace or my joy today, I would have to hand it over to him. And that wasn't happening. Not today.

I also had to continue to remind myself . . . *you're divorced. You're divorced. You're divorced.* But yet so much is still connected. *Divorce is a process . . .* I'm remembering. And this isn't my problem to fix. I'm learning, Father . . . I'm learning . . .

I also had conversations today with two different people who tried to get me to reconsider walking away from this contract. I'm grateful that it would only come after I had such a surety and peace from You. Thank You, Father, that I can trust You. If at any point You want to stop me from walking away from this book offer, You know I'll obey. You will just have to give me as much peace about that decision as You've given me about this one. Because, as of today, I'm walking in the peace of leaving. That peace meter is all I've ever known to follow.

Day 87

I have discovered that I am officially capable of judging in reverse. I didn't even know that was possible, but now I am completely convinced. I was listening to a pastor preach last night, and he was talking about divorce. Of course my ears perked up. "Let's just call it for what it is. Someone isn't willing to do what God has called them to do. God hates divorce. It is the breaking of a covenant. And there is no blessing in that."

All I could hear in those words were "there is no blessing for you. It is over. Finished. Done." It might not have even been what he meant. It was simply what I heard. But I think a lot of it was the way he said it. It brought this spastic applause from one side of the room as if this group had been waiting their entire lives for someone to say something like that so they could applaud. But how many people were sitting there just like me? Needing a little hope. I know we need to hear all messages from Your Word, Father. I honestly do. And I know now more than ever why You hate divorce. And I do know that it is breaking a solemn covenant. But in the middle of where I'm sitting, if I don't temper all things in my life with hope, then I'm going to be in a bad place.

After all, faith is the substance of things hoped for. And without faith I can't please You. So, if I can't even hold on to the hope that You have something for me on the other side of this, then it will be hard to have faith, which in turn will make it impossible to please You.

Does that mean that it makes it more possible to displease You? Does that mean that when my hope is gone I don't care what I do? Sure it does. Even in this situation where there are days when I haven't even wanted to get up or cared if I showered, and just wanted to pull the covers up over my head, way down deep inside of me is a hope that says, *This can't all be for nothing. There has to be something redeemable from this. There has to be a bigger purpose than I know or can see. You really are going to do something good with all of this mess.*

And tonight on the way home, I was so angry with this man. So angry. And yet, I felt You whisper, *Be careful that your freedom doesn't bring you to yet another place of judging others.* And that was when I realized it—that in this new place of understanding and believing . . . and yes, I do believe that there is blessing on the other side of this for me, that I don't become judgmental against those who can't see it. I'm not sure if this man has ever known the pain of divorce. But I have. And I know that without walking it, you are incapable of knowing what you would do in it, or what you can be to those who walk through it.

Help me to not trade one legalistic place for another. Help me to look at this man with as much compassion as I desire him to look at me. I don't want to change Your Word, Father, to fit my circumstance. I don't feel that I have. What I sense tonight is that You have blessing for me. You have purpose for me. And in the middle of all of that, I have to maintain a heart that sees everyone as You do . . . to the best that my simple, human abilities will allow. And, Lord, tonight . . . those are extremely limited.

Day 89

I had a revelation today as I was praying. I'm a huge people pleaser. I know, right . . . a slow learner too. I mean, I knew this, but not to the degree that I practice it or that it harms me. And in that place I am going to have to learn that when I have a check in my gut I don't have to respond right away. Because usually when I do that I'm wanting to respond in the way I think someone else wants me to. But if I do that then, I might not respond in a manner that is reflective of what *You* are saying to me. I'm having to learn that it's okay to say, "I'm not going to give you an answer of how I feel about that right now. I'm going to process it." Then I don't have to backtrack about how I truly feel about something.

People pleasing is tiring, Father. I've done it for so long. I think it is part of the "age" I have worn on my face. Thank You for how sweetly You show me things. Thank You for how graciously You travel with me to the areas of my soul that are distorted and broken, and offer me this huge extension of kindness. Thank You that my heart is willing to let You plow at will. Granted, sometimes it's hard. But it's Your kindness that leads me to repentance. And it leads me to change . . . It's hard to undo all these old ways of doing things. But I'm so desperate for You and so desperate for healing that I'll go anywhere we need to go. Even to the bottom of my stuff.

I got to be at home with Mom and Dad tonight before I fly out to Florida tomorrow. Love it at home. But I couldn't come back here to stay. When the divorce first happened, that was a thought. Just to run back home. But I knew that would be running backward. And I couldn't go backward. I could only move forward. And that's what we've done.

Mom and I had climbed up in her oversized chair and we were talking about how cute Carter is on *Carter Can* on HGTV. I said, "You know, Mom, I'm not 21 anymore." It was a very similar conversation You and I had had the other night. I said, "The girls have headed south; granted I've gained some years back because God is so kind, but I'm not a kid anymore. I probably won't attract what I'm attracted to."

She thought it was far funnier than I did. But I couldn't help but laugh with her. Then You and I had another candid conversation about it tonight . . . how I felt like my best years had been stolen from me. And you once again lovingly reminded me that my best years are ahead. That just like Job (granted I know I'm not Job and have no desire to obtain his status!), his latter years were better than his former. And I feel like that is my promise from You. My latter years are going to be better than my former. And we both know that my girls can always be pointed north again!

Day 90

My flight to Florida this morning was at the crack of dawn. No, it was before the crack of dawn. Dawn had yet to crack. It hadn't even peeked. And I had in no way dressed up for the occasion. I knew I'd have time to go to the hotel and get ready before my signing tonight, so I brushed my hair, put on enough makeup not to scare myself, slipped on a jogging suit and headed to Charlotte to the airport.

When I sat down on the plane, an elderly lady was sitting by the window, with the middle seat between us vacant. She was reading a novel that immediately gave us something to talk about, when someone tapped me on the shoulder. I looked over, and a man was squatting in the aisle next to my seat. He favored Tom Selleck in his *Magnum P.I.* days. I instinctively backed up. He said, "I just noticed you in the airport and I wanted to tell you what a beautiful lady you are." I backed up farther, and he clearly noticed. He stuck out his hand. "I promise I'm not a stalker. I just felt like you needed to know how beautiful you are." And with that he was gone up the aisle to his seat.

The woman next to me said, "I don't think I've ever heard anything as sweet as that." But I knew. I knew it was You. You know exactly what I need, don't You? This man had no idea of our conversation last night. And yet, You let him stop the day to tell me I'm beautiful. To tell me how *You* see me. I'm amazed . . . I'm humbled. I'd say I'm speechless, but obviously we know that doesn't happen often.

You know what it reminded me of? It reminded me of that story where Beth Moore went over and brushed the old man's hair, having no idea why. Not knowing he needed it and yet he couldn't. And that she had made him presentable to see his bride. But You knew what he needed. And You knew what I needed today. And You used a perfect stranger to accomplish it. At least I think he was a stranger . . . even though I never saw him again . . .

Day 94

There is something about the way men look at me that makes me uneasy. There is an element that feels dirty. I've had men notice me through the years, but since my divorce, feeling as if I don't have a place to belong, I don't like the way it feels. Because my heart still feels like it belongs to my husband . . . I just typed "my husband . . ."

You know, I look so much at people's ring fingers now. Men and women. For women, when I see theirs, I wonder what their wedding day was like. What the environment in their home is like. And if a man has a ring, I never let my gaze linger. I feel the need to protect the man from that. He belongs to someone. He deserves the right to not be gawked at or ogled. Granted, I've never been the ogler type. Well, okay, over George Clooney, yes, but that's about it. But the women I've seen with their wedding rings on, especially during this season of travel, have looked so stylish. So put together. As if they are taking a real sense of pride in how they appear. Far different from what we think most married women do. You usually hear, "Once you get married you don't care how you look anymore." But that hasn't been the case here.

In fact, it has been just the opposite. The women I've seen today without wedding rings have looked like they belong on an episode of *What Not to Wear*. Just an interesting observation.

Now, I know there are comfortable moments too, like taking your bra off as soon as you get home, or actually wearing the same outfit two days in a row because it's still laying on the edge of the bathtub where you flung it the night before. Or not washing your hair because you're confident you can "get by" one more day. But even as I write this I am aware of the new place of confidence that I am discovering. And even among all the wedding-band-wearing women on this book tour, I have carried myself as someone who has a place to belong. Because I do. I belong to You. I belong.

Day 96

The email went out this morning to my publisher that I was walking away from the book deal. And by 10:30, both my editor and publisher had called me wanting to talk to me personally instead of to my agent. Then they wanted a conversation with us all together so we could talk through everything and not react so quickly. So I called my editor and told her I felt that was fine. She and I have had such a sweet relationship. We talked about all kinds of things. The points in the contract that were of concern, the issues in communication between my publisher and my agent. Just a lot of different things. It was a kind and good conversation. That's all we've ever had.

But as soon as I got off the phone and realized that opening up dialogue about this would be opening the door again to this contract, I thought I would have a panic attack. The yuck in my gut was real and consuming. That was when I heard that whisper in my heart. *I've already given you your answer.* And You had. To open up dialogue would be as if to say there is the possibility for an answer other than no.

I called my agent and told him what I was feeling. He said, "You have to go with what you feel in your heart, and we will trust that." When he said that, the peace I had had the day I knew I was to walk away settled back over me. I hung up and made one more phone call to Deneen. At first she wanted me to use it as an opportunity to negotiate. But then she stopped and said, "How did you feel when you prayed and the contract came back the way it did?"

I answered immediately. "As if a noose had been removed from my neck that I didn't even know I was wearing."

"Then you clearly have your answer."

I called my editor back and then my publisher. My editor clearly understood because she trusts my heart. And all I can do is trust You. In the natural, none of it makes sense. I don't know if You are simply giving me a season to heal, leading me "beside still waters" for a time and I'll come back to them, or if this is because there is a new season ahead, just like there has been for church and just like this has been for my life.

This feels similar to the day he held the divorce papers in his hand. It is real. It is huge. And it is just You and me now. And in the soul of me is that persistent expectation. And it is of You . . .

✳ ✳ ✳

Ken had an interesting word picture for me today. He was talking about dogs and ticks. I realized really quickly that I have spent years living like a dog that has had ticks sucking off of it—that the life had been sucked out of me, my energy drained, leaving me to feel as if I have had nothing left to give anything else. And that is where I've been.

I remember years ago finding a tick on Maggie. I freaked out because it was huge! And I realized I hadn't even known it was there until I began to pet her one day and ran my hand across it. And now, with all of my stuff exposed, allowing You to place Your hand on areas of my heart and life that have never been touched, You're revealing so much. I've given away so much of what You had placed on the inside of me. I allowed the life to be sucked out of me. Life You gave. I closed my eyes, shut my mouth, denied my true heart; and with that the very life in me was gone. Forgive me. Forgive me for being so unwise with the life You placed in me.

Ken gave me a homework assignment. He asked me to draw a picture of where I desired to see my life in the next five years. My first thought was, *You've obviously never seen me draw.* My second thought was, *I'm trying to figure out where I'm going to be tomorrow.* Fortunately, I had a third thought: *I need to continue to remind myself that there is a tomorrow for me. A good tomorrow.* So it looks like I'm going to be drawing a picture.

Questions

For a lot of people, anger may not feel congruent with who they are. For others, anger may feel too much a part of what they are leaving behind. So, for either of those reasons, when it's time to deal with the anger within your grief, you may want to run in the opposition direction. But dealing with anger is necessary to healing. Are you running from your anger? If so, why do you think you are doing that? What is underneath the anger? By entering into your emotions, what are you afraid will happen? Because moving toward the anger is for the purpose of getting to the emotions underneath. Take those fears, concerns and questions to God and ask Him what is the real truth—His truth—regarding it.

Part of healing, especially in divorce, is to claim our responsibility. If it seems on paper that one partner was "more responsible" for its failure, each of us still has a role. What was your role? How are you beginning to take steps to change those behaviors in your life? And if you haven't yet discovered what your part was, really dig into this in prayer, asking God to clearly show you. Talk with a trusted friend or counselor and don't be afraid to ask the tough questions of yourself.

In loss, there is often the hovering thought that there is something new around the corner. Yet the fear of hurting again can cause you to put up such a shield around your heart that even the entire armed forces couldn't penetrate it. What are your fears about a new relationship? Confessing your fears loosens the enemy's grip. And it's not like you have to worry that God is going to bring you someone tomorrow so you have to be ready. In fact, you can pray and ask Him to protect you until He knows your heart is ready. What walls of protection do you sense you might even now be putting up around your heart? Pray and ask the Lord to help you drop those walls immediately, knowing that He is more than able to protect you.

A judgmental attitude wraps itself in harshness and unteachability. It cloaks itself in the thought process, *If you aren't doing it my way, you're doing it the wrong way.* It is dressed in a prestigious garment of pride and often religion that can be as subtle and as toxic as anything we will ever encounter. In what areas of your life has your heart been judgmental? What are the things about which you could easily adopt a "judgmental in reverse" mentality? Ask God to reveal all that you need to repent of regarding being judgmental. And then keep your heart open to how He wants to begin to give you a new perspective on how you have previously seen things.

Homework

Write an anger list—50 things you are angry about, if you can. After you've written them, find someone to whom you can read the list.

Someone you can trust to handle what comes up in the discovery of those emotions. And don't run from the emotion of it. Feel it. Let it be discovered. Let it be healed. Then invite some friends over and watch *Diary of a Mad Black Woman*. Watch it with an open heart and mind and ask God what He might want to reveal to you through it.

Spend some time remembering God's detailed love to you so far on this journey. Write down the details and use them as a tool for continuing to remember on those days when the enemy would try to convince you that you are off God's radar. It will be a powerful weapon to use against him.

Prayer

I will lift up my eyes to the hills—
where does my help come from?
My help comes from the LORD,
the Maker of heaven and earth.
He will not let your foot slip—
he who watches over you will not slumber;
indeed, he who watches over [put your name here]
will neither slumber nor sleep.
The LORD watches over you-
the LORD is your shade at your right hand;
the sun will not harm you by day,
nor the moon by night.
The LORD will keep you from all harm—
he will watch over your life;
the LORD will watch over your coming and going
both now and forevermore.

PSALM 121, *NIV*

MONTH 4

IT'S OKAY TO GRIEVE . . . STILL
(NOVEMBER)

Day 98

I was doing so well. And then that deep sorrow bore into me. I'm in Jefferson, Texas, for the Books Alive festival tomorrow, and then I'm speaking for the first time since my divorce on Sunday morning. And yet in the middle of the excitement, in the middle of the familiarity of these people I enjoy, I still feel displaced without him. The pastor of the church, my good friend Polly, was talking about sex on our drive over, and all of a sudden that feeling of displacement just swept over me. And once it starts it is like a burst dam.

Then I grieve over the fact that someone new may not want to stop on a road trip and let me go to the bathroom as many times as I have to. And I'm thinking, *The first time some man makes a comment about how much I have to pee, I'm going to freak out!* How I can go from a conversation on sex to how many times I have to pee on a road trip is proof of the indescribable lunacy of pain. Pain makes you crazy.

When I went back to Ms. Joyce's house, who I'm staying with this weekend, and who I love, I climbed in her recliner with her, and as she rocked us, she let me cry and talk and pour out all of my fears. And in the arms of this precious woman who knows her own loss, we grieved together. *We weep with those who weep . . .* thank

You for giving me that tonight. I needed human arms tonight, Father . . . thank You that Ms. Joyce let me climb into hers.

Day 99

I sang in public for the first time in years. Tonight at our book event at The Bull Durham Playhouse in Jefferson, a beautiful young woman named Heather, who has written a powerful book, got up and gave her testimony. She shared her story about being run over by a car when she was little and how she had suffered ever since. There was such a sweet presence of You in that place tonight. As she was talking, the old hymn "Be Still My Soul" ran over and over in my head and my spirit. When she finished giving her testimony and I went up to close out the evening in prayer, I knew I needed to sing this song.

The panic that rose up in me was almost overwhelming. But I knew this was a place of obedience—a place for You to heal just another wound in the vast holes that make up my heart. It wouldn't have mattered if the song meant anything to anyone else in the room, but for me it was another piece of stepping into my freedom—of reclaiming things that *I* had allowed to be stolen, that *I* had handed over. Thank You for giving me the strength to claim them back. Another little step tonight . . . another little step.

Day 100

Thank You for today, Father. I stepped back into the pulpit and you moved so sweetly. After my struggle last week, I nearly called and cancelled. I almost said, "I'm not ready! It's too soon! I don't have anything!" And then You so beautifully gave me John 5:1-9, when Jesus asks the man at the pool of Bethesda, "Do you want to be well?" I know that for me my healing has been my choice. I could have sat by the pool and waited on someone else to push me in, but You came to me and asked me, "Do you want to be well?" And I knew I did.

That's the question You ask each of us, isn't it, because how many of us really don't want to be well? We so identify with our stuff and our pain that to let go of it would be as if we were losing our very identity. There have been so many times in this journey that I have felt like You were stripping me of my very self. Yet as each old piece, like a garment, has fallen away, it has been replaced with another level of healing. And I find that the pain of the stripping leads to the sweet places of my healing. I do want to be well.

Heather's testimony right before my message was such a perfect reflection of that truth. You placed in her this tenacity of spirit to fight for her healing. Not just her physical healing, but also the healing of her heart and her soul. And as the message layered against her story, You whispered as I sat down, *You do hear me.* And I wept.

You know how important hearing You is to me. It is essential to all that I do, but for me it is more than that. It is a desperate place. Maybe it's out of a place of fear that isn't healthy. I'm still digging into that to see if the response is more out of my legalistic background or out of a reverential fear of not wanting to miss You. But I don't have to figure all of that out today; what I do know today is that I hear You. I heard You here. And I have been hearing You. And You are in the middle of this journey in such a sweet way. It gave me peace about the huge decision I made this week. And it gives me peace going into my future. I do want to be well. And I am learning so beautifully what that looks like . . .

Day 101

I got home from Jefferson today and had to go pick up my girls. He had kept them for me. When I saw him, he wrapped me in his arms and hugged me. I miss his arms. I miss him holding me. I really do. Then tonight there was a horrible storm, and he called to check on me. We talked for about 30 minutes, and he shared some personal things with me. And in the conversation my heart ached at how we had come to this. I so didn't want this . . . I just wanted my home. Becoming divorced . . . just another piece.

Day 102

You asked me another tough question today, Father. When I was praying about a friend who is in a huge financial crisis—a debt of over half a million dollars—my heart was overcome with emotion for her. I spoke out loud while I was praying, "Lord, if I had that half a million dollars I would give it to her and pay off all of her debt." Then Your question came up in my heart: *But would you give her all that you have?*

It caught me off guard. It was clear. And loud. And required a response. You know I've always been a giver. I've probably given sometimes when I shouldn't have because that is how my heart is geared. So, to hear a question like that often makes me question myself. I asked You to confirm to me if this was really You or just my overly compassionate heart. And by the end of the day, You had confirmed it completely. When I laid my head on my pillow, the decision wasn't a question of whether or not I would give it to her; that issue was settled—as clearly settled as the issue of my book deal. I would give away all that I had. For one reason, and one reason alone: You were asking me to. The question in my head as I lay down tonight was not whether or not I would, but how . . .

Day 103

A friend of mine came over tonight. She is a realtor. She and I began to talk about listing my home. We have had it *For Sale by Owner* since the sign went up in the yard in May. And as we began to talk, all I could see was my savings and everything we had worked for being taken away. I had no idea how there would be anything left to purchase a home for myself. And as the fear was flying all around me, I clearly knew why You were asking me to trust You with my money in a way I never had before.

For these past 13 years I have trusted in his ability to produce and provide. But now I have to completely trust You. Though I knew You were always our provision, there was still this element of depending on him. And I realized when I felt the panic sweep over me the grip that money still has on me. I feel that You are letting me know that just as You have asked me to trust You with my life by letting go of my marriage, and to trust You with my calling by letting go of my book deal, I am now being asked to trust You with my finances by letting it sift through my fingers to someone else simply because You ask. And I said, "Yes." No, I said, "YES!"

Day 105

We had a sweet time this morning, didn't we, Father. I was listening to T. D. Jakes. He's been a companion without knowing it through this journey. These are some of the words that I felt You speak to me through him today. *That this place I am today is a place where You will bless me. This is an "enlarging my courts" place, a "lengthening my stakes" place, a "getting ready for You to pour me out blessings" place, and every idol has to be removed in order for any of that to happen.* And I feel that I have done that to the best of my ability here, Father.

I sensed You saying, *It's a breakthrough.* That when I finally start enlarging my places, You command a blessing. A blessing of an open door, of healing, of joy, of peace in my mind, of deliverance in my spirit, a way out, of being the head and not the tail. I can't die here, Father, even though there have been days when death would be welcomed. But You're not finished with me. You have been making me restructure so You can make room for what You are going to restore.

T. D. said, "He didn't create vegetation. He just spoke to the dirt and said, 'Bring forth.' God knows what's in you and he is commanding you to bring it out. He spoke to the water and said, 'Bring forth,' and fish were born. Wonder what God can bring out of you! But there is some stuff in you that's got to come out."

Father, there is so much that the canker worm and the locust have eaten up in my life, and so much left to come out. But I believe this is my year to bring forth. But first the seed must die right . . . that is what all of this surrender has been for. Seed is dying so a harvest can come forth.

Day 110

For my entire adult life I have protested paying any attention to the leaves during the fall. When Dad pastored in Charleston, he would take the "senior saints" on fall foliage excursions to the mountains, and it just always wreaked of mothballs and cheap perfume. So I have refused it any part of my yearly experience. But today it refused me. It refused to be ignored. I was driving to the doctor and there was this unavoidable display of breathtaking color I'm not sure I have ever seen before. It was magenta and kiwi, it was mustard and blood orange, and it was gorgeous.

Immediately my mind goes to the question, "Did You create the trees from green to the colors, or did You start off deciding what colors the trees would be in the fall and then work Your way backward?" Either way You have outdone Yourself. And it has arrested me. Reminding me once again that creation really does declare Your handiwork. And it was so like You to put it right there for me to enjoy.

What was so interesting was that at that exact moment I was praying, asking You to show me the "deep and hidden things." I've been memorizing this verse in Daniel 2:22 and I have been asking You that so much. And then as I'm praying, these leaves start falling from the trees, and I'm captured by this breathtaking color. And just like those colors are hidden for six months of the year and then You bring them out from hiding and allow our hearts to be impacted by their beauty, You spoke something of Your "hidden secrets" to my heart.

I sensed You speak that this fall was going to be a season of more things falling away and that when winter came it was going to be a season to hibernate and continue to heal, and that when spring arrived there was going to be a real sense of newness of life for me. And I just receive that, Lord. I receive that as a hidden piece from You.

Ken wanted to see my picture today. I even found it interesting what I had drawn. I had folded my paper in half to draw on two sides. On one side I drew what I felt was reflective of my calling. Two bookshelves like you would see at any bookstore—one of them holding my latest fiction book and another holding my first nonfiction book, neither of which at this moment are even an immediate reality. The other side held something that wasn't a much better drawing than when I had stick figured it out in middle school. But it was a picture of a house and a family. Each side depicted the deepest places of my soul.

Ken looked at them and asked me to tell him about them. I did. I told him they were representative of my heart's greatest desires. He didn't have a lot to say, making it clear that the exercise was more about staying engaged with my heart than needing an answer. I think sometimes I am so prone to wanting to make sure I have the right answer . . . to performing . . . that I have forgotten to live, to dream. This helped me stay focused on the latter.

But as he looked at my picture, he finally looked up at me and said, "I want you to start thinking about what another person may fill inside of you that your former husband didn't." It was an interesting question, one I've traveled to at moments but not sat in. And yet it's one that provides an excitement to think about what You have waiting for me. Oh, my side—I just said meeting someone provides a sense of excitement.

❋ ❋ ❋

I mailed the check off today. My bank account is now completely empty, and I've never had a more perfect peace that You are my provider. Everything I have is Yours, Father . . . everything.

Day 117

I've been pretty uneasy today. I'm home in South Carolina for the holidays, and I'm feeling anxious. But just as You have done so preciously, You speak to my heart. I'm reading Philip Yancey's book on prayer, and I read a story about this family who was in a situation because of persecution where they could no longer pray or talk about the Lord and how, in spite of that, all five of their children still came to know God. And once again I realized that You have everything that concerns me in the palm of Your hand. So once again I give all of my anxieties to You. No matter what the rest of this year may hold. No matter what tomorrow may hold, I am in the palm of Your hand . . .

Day 118

Today is Thanksgiving. My first Thanksgiving since the divorce. I'm not sure why, but I haven't really been dreading the holidays. Anxious, but not full of dread. That could be two-fold. We were separated over the holidays five years ago. And that was so fresh and those holidays were so painful. But now I'm getting used to this new way of life, so thankfully that fresh pain isn't there. At least it's not today. We all know that could change tomorrow with my track record. But I prayed that I would be okay when I got back home, because on top of that, I'd be PMS-ing . . . Don't you love that!

This was also the day he proposed to me. He proposed to me on Thanksgiving, 15 years ago. But even that doesn't seem to hurt today.

In all honesty, remembering has been my friend lately. Remembering the pain of how I got here has been my friend. And I think it has helped remove some of the dread of today. In fact, I'm looking forward to the peace of this holiday season. So, there really is so much that I'm simply thankful for today, Father. I'm thankful for how You've walked with me through this dark journey. I'm thankful for Your continued presence. I'm grateful that You have both him and me in the palm of Your hand and that You have a future for both of us. I'm thankful that You have revealed Yourself to me in so many ways this year, including the deep and hidden things. And I'm believing that You are going to continue to touch me in the deep places of my life.

Be with my friends today, Lord, those who are hurting from divorce, those who have lost their spouses to death this year, those who are lonely and hungry and desperate. Be with each person who needs a reminder of Your love today. And be with him. Yes, be with him . . .

And be with my family as we celebrate You and Your love and Your goodness. I'm thankful for so much, Lord . . . I'm thankful for so much.

Day 120

Lord, I can't thank You enough for how wonderful this week has been. I haven't shed one tear. Is that a miracle, or what! Thanksgiving was a wonderful day; and honestly, every day I've been home has been perfect. You have continued to be so faithful to me during this season, and I can't thank You enough. I know there are final decisions to be made when I get home. I know that I have to decide what church is going to be my home, and I really sense in my heart that it is The Journey unless You show me otherwise. All I know is that it has provided this beautiful place of healing for my soul, and I feel like my gifts could be used there. Guide me, I pray. Lead me and open and close the doors of my life as You see fit . . . and thank You again for allowing this big holiday to come and go without the tears. For today I am simply grateful for the absence of tears.

Questions

The expectations for grief to end quickly can be so strong. When friends no longer call to check in, family doesn't quite understand why the grief remains, but the silence inside the walls of your house can scream a reminder of what once was and yet is no longer. Are you still grieving? What does that look like for you? What are you grieving now that you weren't grieving two months ago? Know that it is okay. Remember, grief has no playbook. This is your journey. Invite God right into the center of it.

Are there some places of faith during this season that God is asking you to step out in? What are they? What are you feeling about them? Scared? Anxious? Uncertain? Yet obedience brings with it a sweet peace—a peace that surpasses all of our understanding. Take that step and see what waits for you on the other side of obedience.

In this new season of your life, what have you had to surrender? Have you been reluctant or do you know that you can trust God with anything? Are there other things He may be asking you to surrender? Spend some time with Him, asking Him to clearly show you your heart and anything you may need to let go of.

What are some of your secret desires? Write them down. Your Father already knows them, but maybe you need to see them more clearly. Do you believe He desires to give you your secret desires? Pay attention during this season to how He answers even those "secret desires."

Homework

Okay, let's get creative. Draw a picture of where you see your life five years from now. Remember, this is about getting you to believe again that God truly does have something for you outside of this place of grief. This is not the whole of your story; it is only a piece of it.

Spend a day outside, taking in whatever season it is. And I mean, take it in. If it is summer, go to the beach, grab a picnic lunch and head out to a park. If it is spring, take a walk or grab a convertible and go for a drive without a destination. If it is fall, take a drive and look at the changing color of the leaves. Grab some spiced tea and inhale it deeply. If it is winter, bundle up and get out there and watch your breath flow from your body. Feel the cold against your skin. Drink some hot chocolate and don't worry about the calories. Take in the sights, the sounds, the feelings and the beauty of the season that is around you. And ask God to speak to your heart something from His "deep and secret things." Listen . . . and don't ever forget what He tells you in this moment.

Prayer

The heavens tell of the glory of God. The skies display his marvelous craftsmanship. Day after day they continue to speak; night after night they make him known. They speak without a sound or a word; their voice is silent in the skies; yet their message has gone out to all the earth, and their words to all the world. The sun lives in the heavens where God placed it. It bursts forth like a radiant bridegroom after his wedding. It rejoices like a great athlete eager to run the race. The sun rises at one end of the heavens and follows its course to the other end. Nothing can hide from its heat. The law of the Lord is perfect, reviving the soul. The decrees of the Lord are trustworthy, making wise the simple. The commandments of the Lord are right, bringing joy to the heart. The commands of the Lord are clear, giving insight to life. Reverence for the Lord is pure, lasting forever. The laws of the Lord are true; each one is fair. They are more desirable than gold, even the finest gold. They are sweeter than honey, even honey dripping from the comb.

PSALM 19:1-10, *NLT*

MONTH 5

BECOMING ALIVE

(DECEMBER)

Day 127

"What can I pray for?" Ken asked, as he has each time I've sat across from him for the last seven months.

I hesitated.

"What's wrong?"

"I feel like I'm floundering."

"I can sense that." He took his usual prayer position, sitting back in his chair, hands folded. And I took mine. I leaned over on my knees and bowed my head.

He prayed. "And, Lord, if Denise is floundering because You are taking her from a pond to a lake, then may she rest in the floundering."

That so struck me. It resonated with me intensely. Near the end of my session he came back to that. "Did you hear what I prayed?"

"Yeah, I did. And it really struck me."

"I really believe that for you." His blue eyes were transparent with his sincerity. "You're not big enough to thwart God's plan, you know."

I had to sit in that. There was so much weight in that for me. Because I know me. My biggest fear is missing You. My biggest fear is getting it wrong and missing what You have for me. As if there is this huge box filled with all of Denise's promises, and if I make one wrong move, then it will be as if I pass my box on by and there is no chance to redeem it. This is my religious piece, isn't it Father? You are going to rid me of my religious spirit. Because I have spent my life believing this lie. And it is so contrary to all You have shown me over these last nine months in this journey with You. Ken's one statement felt as if it lifted the weight of the world off of me . . . "my burden is light." Yeah, it is, isn't it.

I got up to leave and felt as if I was all but wearing the freedom his statement had just given me. He could see it in me, and he smiled. "I can think of so many people I'd like to introduce you to," he said.

I laughed and held up my hand.

"I know. Not yet."

Day 130

I was a kid tonight. And I was completely alive. Almost a year ago I planned this trip with my mom; my surrogate sister, Joan, who was my matron of honor at my wedding; her mom, Jean, and her mother-in-law, Doris; and two of her girlfriends, Kathy and Cheryl. We scheduled a three-day Disney Cruise and two days at Disney World. And tonight I was a kid. There is something magical about Disney World, when you walk up that main street and see that little piece of Disney magic. And as we did, my heart was completely alive.

But it was Space Mountain that proved it. Joan and I, and her two friends, left our mothers in a store, being taken care of by a really sweet sales clerk, and headed for Space Mountain. Because the park clears out and only a certain number of tickets are sold to Mickey's Very Merry Christmas party, the line was minimal. After that first exhilarating race through darkness, we came out like giddy school girls. The only thing we each knew is that we wanted to do it all over again. So we did. And we shamelessly took three eight-year-olds to a footrace to get to the line first. By the time we got off the second time the kid at the end of the ride who helps you get out of your cart told us a back way to go so we could get to the front of the line quicker without having to go outside. I had the brief idea of grabbing him and kissing him, but it would have taken us that much longer to get back on the ride.

After what I think was five childlike trips, we finally made it back to our mothers and headed to find a spot to watch the Christmas parade. As the lights danced down Main Street, and the biggest noisemaker next to the music was the laughter of children, my heart was completely and wonderfully alive. I didn't want to leave. I honestly could have spent the entire night taking in every nuance, every twinkling light, magical smell, wonderful childlike expression and not let it go. But I didn't. I simply memorized them. And even now I can see them.

As we made our final stroll down Main Street to head out of the gate of the Magic Kingdom, I was pushing Miss Doris, Joan's mother-in-law, who had just gotten two new hips, in her wheelchair that we made her get for two reasons: first, because it would have taken us the entire evening to get to Space Mountain, and second—and I'm more than willing to admit it—having her in that wheelchair shamelessly got us to the front of the line quicker. So, as we were laughing and singing our way down Main Street, I had an idea. I took off with Miss Doris in that wheelchair and pushed her like a speed racer. I twirled her. I did a wheelie with her. I scared the heebie-jeebies out of her, and we all laughed until we were crying. I think one of them actually wet her britches . . . thus clearly identifying the age group I was with.

So, Father, I'm laying my head down tonight with such a child-like sense of wonder. Mom is in the bathroom taking off her makeup, and I am thinking of how even almost a year ago You knew how desperately my heart would need to feel the wonder of a child today. How indescribably detailed is Your love. And tonight You reminded me once again why You desire us to come to You like little children. Because children have reckless abandon, endless stamina and completely open hearts. And I don't know one of those things that You can't work through beautifully. Becoming divorced . . . just another piece of the journey.

Day 132

Mom can't swim. I think that is why for the last two days she has been dreading the cruise. I'm not even sure she enjoyed the last two days at Disney. But that all changed when she stepped onto this ship. I wish I could have captured the look on her face. To be in your sixties and see something for the first time, and have the awe and wonder of a child, has to be one of the most beautiful sights to witness. And I got to see it today. On the face of my mom . . . it was priceless.

Once we got Miss Doris and her two new hips away from setting off the metal detector, and got Mom away from the 80-year-old man with the shiny gold tooth who propositioned her, we walked through the doors of the ship. As we slipped into the breathtaking three-story foyer, Disney characters were all around, welcoming us. We had gotten an early lunch seating, so we walked straight into the dining room and immediately sat down for an indescribable spread of food.

Mom could hardly take it all in. All she kept saying was "your dad would love this . . . your dad would love this." Her heart went straight to its desire to share this moment with her life companion. And my heart had the privilege of sharing this with You. And share it we did. Every bite. Every sound. Every look of wonderment . . . of Mom's and mine, I got to share it all with You.

Day 133

What a great day! We landed at Nassau where they have their straw market and every fake handbag known to mankind. I mean, you've never seen so many Louis Vuittons, Guccis, Coaches . . . it was a plethora of faux leather that few will ever get the privilege of inhaling. We meandered through the wanton wears, and then Mom and I went back to the ship and took Miss Doris to the theater to see *Enchanted.* It was a far better theater experience than when we had taken my nieces a few weeks earlier to the old theater in my mom's hometown, with the horrible seats, terrible sound and big scratches in the screen. This was paradise. Yet not quite good enough to keep Sister Doris awake. Because somewhere between singing rats and dresses made from curtains, Sister Doris was snoring.

After the movie, I sneaked away for some time by myself in the rainforest spa and actually fell asleep for a little while. I woke up in time to join the old girls for bingo. I love bingo! I've loved it ever since I won over $300 on a cruise he and I took about 12 years ago. And today I won a pot of $127, but unfortunately, I had to split it with two other women. I think Miss Jean was a little peeved at me because she always wins at bingo. Mom sat there and watched us but didn't play. I have a sneaking suspicion she is convinced it is gambling. But she was tickled to death when I won. Next thing on my agenda is getting her to Las Vegas!

On the way to dinner I was carrying one of my small purses. I said something to Mom about all of the purses he had bought me. And the thought struck me that he would never buy me another gift. And that weight collided with my heart. Then, as we sat in the theater to watch the evening performance, I looked around at all of these families. The kids were sitting up in their seats with this childlike amazement, and I thought of the family I should have at this point. And don't. There was so much in this entire evening that forced still-embedded pockets of grief to bobble to the surface and pop open.

But it wasn't all grief. Joan and I found the nightclub. Yep, on a Mickey Mouse boat! Actually, it was an adults-only "lounge," with music . . . and adults! There are moments when I love adults . . . We sat down and I ordered me a Coke, and they got to the business of what we had gone for. It was scavenger hunt night! And we were raring to go. The host for the evening laid down the ground rules, which were pretty nonexistent. It was basically whoever got to him first with what he was asking for, and did it the most times, won. How hard could that be?

He started with the basic stuff—lipstick, baseball cap (didn't have that)—then he got a little more creative. "I want you to bring me a man with women's lipstick and women's shoes." Well, seeing as we were manless, we grabbed the first waiter we saw, slapped some of Joan's lipstick on him and my size 6 shoes on his size 11 feet and sent him running. We got that one first! And somewhere in the middle of it all I was out of breath and my stomach ached from the laughter. And I saw how You are able to be present in everything. Some think they can find You only in the reverent. Some think You are only found in churches and synagogues and cathedrals. Some think You are only found in the Bible or in praise and worship music. I think I thought that once . . . but I have found You in "the land of the living." Like David found You when he said, "I would have lost heart, unless I had believed I would see the goodness of the Lord in the land of the living" (Ps. 27:13, *NKJV*). I have found You in movies and love songs. I have found You in dancing and singing. I have found You in bingo games and scavenger hunts. I have found You in the places where I live. Because in each one of these moments my heart has been fully connected to You.

Father, I have spent so many years being so wrapped up in how I thought You should move, where I thought You should move, how spiritual I needed to be for You to move, and I am learning that in my simple, obedient, daily act of living, You move. In learning what my heart looks like, and in allowing it to be alive, You are moving. And I am grateful. Tonight You moved in an adults-only club on a Disney Cruise ship. You moved me to laughter and You moved me to tears. And in the middle of it all, You fed my soul with a sweet manna. A daily bread. And I noticed. You are gracious to refuse my ability to miss You.

Day 134

Oh my . . . I think I had the best lunch today that I have ever had. We spent the day on Disney's Private Island, Castaway Key, that came fully equipped with a Christmas tree when we walked off of the boat. But the lunch . . . oh, the lunch. Thank You, God, that food will be in heaven. I had a little sampling of everything— the burger, the fish, the chicken, all of it. Every bite was perfect.

We laid out, and then we girls went on a Banana Boat ride. I was scared to death. I almost backed out. Yes, I almost backed out on a Banana Boat ride. Pitiful, I know. But ever since I took my

Sunday School class white-water rafting, I have been deathly afraid of rides in water. I don't even like going on boats anymore. That's why I was so petrified when I went out with Mark and Deneen on theirs. But I made myself go. And honestly, I can't even tell you that I enjoyed it. But I did it. And in that was my victory. And I think I had fun. I mean, once it was over I was ready to do it again. I think if I could have ridden it about five times I would have been fearless. But I did it. One more thing I have been afraid to do that I faced head-on. Must be a theme, huh . . .

At dinner tonight, Doris cracked me up. She whistled for the waiter. She whistled . . . at the waiter. Like, "Hey, you, come here now!" kind of whistle. I told Joan, "You just can't take them out anymore, can you!" We cracked up. Then we headed to the evening's show and again the children in the audience captured me. But it was different tonight. Tonight I was captured by their awe. What awes us? So few things anymore. I remember years ago, before he and I got married, we went to a Gary Smalley marriage conference, and Gary talked about how we should have awe for our spouse. And yet so few of us live with a sense of awe over anything, let alone the people who live under our roof. But these babies were awed. And, Father, You have so awed me this year . . .

Joan and I got Darlyn in the Disney Night club tonight, and I am so not joshing you! My mom, in a nightclub! I thought I had done something incredible the first time I got her to go into my favorite dive, Leo's, in her hometown, that has the best chicken wings ever, and had her sitting under the Bud Light sign. Yep, I thought that was huge. But this! This was priceless. Joan and I, however, got gypped again. We so should have won the Scavenger Hunt tonight. We were even armed and ready to go. We had an extra bra stuck in Joan's handbag, just in case that was on the list of items. And we still didn't win!

There was a man in there tonight with a girl. When I headed back to my seat from delivering one of our items to our judge, the Entertainment Coordinator, I looked up to find this man staring at me. Not the "just happened to look up and you were there" kind of stare, but the "I'm taking you in" kind of stare. And he already had a date. I focused my attention back on Joan and Mom and my Coke. But all I could think in that moment was, "Father, please let the man you bring me always respect me with the way he takes other people in."

I know that beauty is appreciated. Trust me, I can appreciate a good-looking man. But there is a look that degrades, a look that wounds, a look that betrays. Even as I write this I can tell that my wounds still run deep here. So, Father, let me always show the level of respect that I desire to receive. And when you're picking him out, may he honor me in this way.

Joan and Kathy and I decided we were going to pretend we were teenagers and stay up all night, because we didn't want to miss anything. So first we went to the midnight buffet. We didn't want to stand in the long line, but we did get crepes. Then, after we sent our mothers to bed and Joan's other friend, we ordered us some French fries, simply because we could, went up to the top deck and got us some Coke and ate up. We talked and laughed and enjoyed each other, and then we went and laid out on lounge chairs on the deck and just talked as the wind whipped around us with the cool night air. Eventually, we went in to check on Joan and Kathy's roommate, and that was when our age hit us and we realized that we had only been "pretending" to be teenagers.

Well, okay, my age hit me, and I decided I needed rest. I think Joan and Kathy could have stayed up all night long. But I went on back to my room. I don't want to see it end, Father. Honestly, I don't. I wish I could stay in this place forever. I've had this beautiful moment to forget everything that is back home. For six days I have been completely allowed to forget that life as I know it isn't back there. But You are . . . thankfully . . . You are. And You also have given me new memories . . . just like I prayed for. New memories are replacing old ones.

Day 135

I came home today, and he picked me up. I was so wishing that I hadn't orchestrated it this way. I was dreading this from the moment I woke up. Everyone else was going home to the airport, and their husbands were going to pick them up; but I was going to be picked up by a man who is no longer my husband. But with all things that are You, You gave me solace in that moment. You gave me the ability to see the broken places that so deeply remain. And when my heart wanted to ache, you gave it the ability to recognize that some things in the past you just can't go back to . . .

Tonight I was studying my book on divorce. The writer was talking about how the things that you do should be of interest to the person that you fall in love with. I don't know that I've ever truly known that. I've said so much over the last few months about feeling known, and I was in a lot of ways, but in the deep ways, I wasn't. Not truly known. Father . . . thank You for how You know me. Thank You that I am known by You. And thank You that when and if You bring someone, he will care about the things that matter to me.

You know that I'm about to go on this fast starting in January. And I'm still reflecting on what I felt like You spoke to my heart about the leaves falling and the hibernation of winter and the new birth of spring. And I'm asking, Father, that during this fast that I would clearly hear You. Will You speak insight into my life and heart during this season of grief, as You have been? Will You give me a fresh word? A word of encouragement and advancement for this coming year? I truly have faith that great things are ahead for me and for this new year. Honestly, I'm believing for great things.

Day 140

Ten days until Christmas. It's amazing how many emotions I go through. Last night, riding in the car, I was thanking You that the heavy grief was gone. I was thanking You that the deep pain was gone. Even though I have moments of tears, I haven't felt that drop-to-the-floor weight for almost a month. But then today sweeps in and I wake up alone and I know that the day will be spent alone. The house can get so quiet, Father. But when I get so overcome, I think of women walking through this same pain with children, and I have no idea how they do it. And I'm grateful that as deep as the ache for children has been through the years, I wouldn't want them here. Not in this. Yet, ask those who have children who go through this process and they will say they don't know how they'd get through without them. Which all proves that our journeys are individual and that You know exactly what we need.

I don't know why I've been allowed to walk this journey this way. It is nothing but Your grace. Yet in writing that it causes me to ask, "But if someone else's journey looks different, does that mean Your grace is less for them?" Even as I ask that I come back to the thought that I am basing these thoughts on an earthly perspective of what is right and wrong. I'm basing this on the human thought process of what is fair. But you deal in a completely different realm—a realm that doesn't operate on fairness as we view fairness, but on a principle that knows what is best for each of Your children. I think that is what I came away with the other day when I was with Ken.

I told him that there were days I have felt guilty for the life You have allowed me to lead over these past few months.

"Why?" he asked.

"Because other people's journeys look different."

"But when God made you, He knew how to get the best out of you. And so He is loving you in this journey with what is best for you."

Yet there are days when I don't feel like You have gotten the best out of me. Even lately I've felt so unproductive with myself.

It's like since I took that time off at Thanksgiving, and then the cruise, I haven't even wanted to work. Yet, I still do. I always do what I need to do. And You are so faithful to me that way.

But I do ache, Father. I think of him often and ache. And I also think quite often of what falling in love again will look like. Last night I was walking into the movie theater, the air was so cold on my face, and I was looking at all of the Christmas lights, and I felt this sense of newness inside of me. A freedom somehow. I would have stayed married forever, Father, if You hadn't drawn a line.

Yet now there is a fear that I could fall in love again one day and wake up and he has simply decided he doesn't love me anymore. There are just no guarantees. But, Lord, You are a guarantee. And I know that if I am patient, prayerful and faithful, You will bring the man You have created for this next season of my life, who will love me as I have loved—that I am going to reap what I have sown in regard to love. Thank You for this promise to my heart. Thank You that You know my heart's desire and that You have a good plan for me.

Thank You that Christmas will be wonderful, and laughter will be in abundance and Your Word will flow out of me when I speak at Dad's church over the holiday, because I can hear You. Even when I don't think I can, You remind me that I can. And even when I mess up, You can still bring me back to the goodness of the land where I belong. What a sweet umbrella of grace You have for me . . . what a sweet umbrella of grace . . .

Day 143

All day I have felt "lovey." I mean LOOOVVVVVVVEEEEYY. It was the word I would use in my marriage in those moments when I desired to be loved intimately. And it hung around all day. So tonight I went with Sarah to watch Celine Dion's final concert at Cesar's at the theater. On the way home I began to realize that You can handle any conversation I need to have. And tonight we needed to have a conversation about my overactive hormones. Yet

I started by thanking You that those feelings were still alive in me, given how I had to shut them down. And that tonight those feelings didn't have to be repressed but could be communicated to You. I'm not sure I realized how You truly can handle everything. That every piece of my heart is safe with You, even the most vulnerable and intimate. Thank You that You are a husband to the husbandless. And tonight You let me carry one of my deepest longings straight to Your throne. You talked me through my pain and testosterone . . .

Day 145

When I met with Ken today I shared with him how I was trying to discern what signs might have been there in my dating season that I should have noticed, and that whether consciously or unconsciously, I avoided them or simply didn't notice them.

He said, "It's okay to notice those things and to think about that now, but you can't use that to think that when you meet someone they can't have any issues, because then, it is almost as if you are using this knowledge as ammunition. You know, it is the illusion that gets you through the disillusionment. Marriage has its peaks and valleys."

"And it's hurricanes and typhoons," I said. We laughed. "You know though, after 13 years of marriage I was really enjoying it. Being married. Even with all of the things that were wrong, I was enjoying the sweet place of being married."

"I can believe that."

"But I am beginning to feel alive."

"Yeah? What's that look like?"

"Wheeling an old woman down Main Street at Disney World." He laughed. "Yeah."

"And you know what else I discovered? I was thinking the other day about when I wrote my first Savannah book. It was like God was so desperate to get my heart back that He gave me this character Savannah. She was so abandoned and free. Like I used to be. And in writing her story, it was as if He was trying to remind me of who I really was and what I had walked away from. Because I had let so much be shut down. As if I was afraid to be myself. I didn't even sing anymore, and now I do it all the time. It's as if I was living through her. She was a gift."

"He was wooing you."

The revelation of that fell hard. "Yes, He was wooing me."

"He will woo us or push us toward Him, you know."

"I didn't get it until He pushed. I wished I would have listened to the wooing."

"Feel's better living for yourself now though, doesn't it?"

"You can't imagine," I said, and paused. My thoughts immediately went back to my marriage. "Ken, what do you look for when you're choosing a mate? I'm not even sure I know anymore."

"You know, whoever God sends you will do just what you were describing for you. He will accentuate that feeling of being alive in you, not push it down. And you should bring out that same feeling in him. And you should also always look for someone who is continually willing to grow and change."

"That's good."

He leaned back and smiled and nodded the way he does. "Yeah. You know what else I would do . . . I would get a journal that is nothing but for those moments that make you feel alive."

That was easy. I came straight home and pulled out a beautiful gray suede journal I have with pink outlined birds on it and began my "alive journal." I felt like I was 12 years old with a glue stick, and loved every minute of it. What better memories to capture than those where your heart has been awakened to the fact that it is actually still beating . . .

We're having a girl! Yep . . . well, Damon and Sarah are having a girl. And good thing, because I can do girls. Darren and Janey have given me three nieces, and I know what to do with them. Boys, not so much. To be this close to Christmas, and know. Now we can buy stuff just for her. Who cares about Damon and Sarah anymore . . . Christmas is going to be about Georgia! That's her name. Love it . . .

have a fondness for it. And so grateful, Father, for this other sweet piece of healing.

Day 146

I was having dinner with my friend Karol tonight. I was telling her about my alive journal and how I was beginning to feel like I actually was alive. She said, "When I first met you at the Titan's football game, you looked so much older than you do now."

How many times have I heard that? And look at what You are doing for me. Just as I've prayed, You are restoring even my natural years that the enemy was able to steal. May I not allow him to steal anything else.

Day 148

I had my first really sad moment in a while. Sarah called to tell me she could feel the new baby inside of her. I'm so excited, Father. I really am. This whole journey of waiting on this little one's arrival and knowing it will be here for me to enjoy is almost more than I can ask for. And it feels so healing. When I got off the phone I thanked You that one day that may be a part of my story. But I also was sad that I never shared it with him. Yet I know we could have still ended up here. And I wouldn't want that for a child. Not my child anyway. And it has been a blessing for my journey that I haven't had to carry a child's pain as well. Thank You, Lord, that You know how You make us, and You know what is best for each one of our stories. And this is how You chose to write mine.

Day 150

It's Christmas Eve. My Maggie's thirteenth birthday. She has been such a gift to me. I'll never forget her being handed to me my first married Valentine's in that tiny bag from Crystal's Jewelry store. We were at Opryland Hotel where he had a concert. We let her walk around the floor and she took a poop right there. We brought her home to our tiny two-bedroom apartment and put her in a box in the kitchen where she cried until he went and put one of his T-shirts in the box with her. She has been an independent and obstinate creature ever since. I wanted her to be a lap dog. She wanted nothing to do with it. I wanted her to be a lover. She has been an "I'll let you know if I need you" kind of girl.

But when the tears would come she'd appear from nowhere and let me love her. I've cried more tears into that cream-colored fur then you could count. But when I was done she'd go right back to the mentality that she had just done me a favor.

She loves treats too. Dang, she loves food in general. She loves men too. Especially her Uncle D.D. She also has the biggest bug eyes you'll ever see and the most crooked teeth I've ever witnessed on a dog, which are highly exaggerated because of her extreme underbite. She looks mad at the world most days, but that face can melt my heart. And she's had a kick in her step since we got to Nana and Granddaddy's. I think it's because she has her new haircut and feels like she has been liberated. Of course I think she's cold too, because she shakes all the time. But when I put her Frosty sweater on her she refuses to walk. I mean she stands there like arthritis has stricken her paralyzed. If she does take a step it is so labored you would think she was hastening to glory in the next few moments. It is hysterical! And she's my girl.

It's been a really sweet couple of days, Father. Thank You too for the moments when I sense my aloneness in the practical ways of living . . . when there's no one to drive me to the airport. When there's no one to get my mail or put out my trash or watch over my home while I'm gone. When there's no one to drop me off at the door of the church on days when it's excruciatingly cold or rainy, You are still with me. And watch over me to perform Your word in my life; and thank You for how You already have.

Well, once again You have amazed me. Dad had sent the word out that whatever my family did they weren't to get me anything that would make me cry. Whoever would dream a kitchen appliance could accomplish that? No one knew about my jar issue. You know, my can of sweet potato preserves that I couldn't open. The incident that led me to admit that I was angry and write 50 reasons why. Well, tonight when I was opening my gifts from Damon and Sarah, there was this odd little gadget on the top of the packages. So when I took it off of the package and read what it was I burst into tears. It was a jar opener for hard-to-open lids. Did you hear that? For hard-to-open lids!

My dad said, "What in the world did you get her?!"

Damon threw his hands up in the air. "It's a blasted jar opener! How could I make her cry with a jar opener!"

When I finally quit blubbering, I told them the story. By the time I was through we were all crying. Even right now, lying here talking to You, it is still easy for the anger to settle on me that I have to open my own jars; and with it surfaces that obstinate desire to always do it so no one can ever leave me again trying to figure out how to do it alone. But to live there would negate all the beauty of Your detailed love—the detailed love that You have shown me in this journey we've taken together.

You have shown me once again that there is nothing You can't or won't do for me that will meet my needs. "My God will supply all your needs according to His riches in glory in Christ Jesus" (Phil. 4:19, *NASB*). You have been the ultimate supplier all year. You have met me in my darkest places. You have captured my heart and soul and proven so faithful to me. And You have shown me that You can get to me whatever You have for me. I don't have to worry about how You'll do it or when You'll do it. I'm on Your radar, and every need I have You already see and know. You amaze me, Father. The details of Your love continually amaze me.

Day 151

It's Christmas morning, Father. And I'm alive. Yep, one more holiday almost over. One more marker about to be marked. One more new memory to create to erase an old one. Don't need stuff today, Father. Really never have. You have given me all I need. The reminder last night was enough. You see me. You know where I am. You know me by name.

So, can I thank You today? Can I thank You for daring to step from heaven and come to dwell here on earth, knowing what Your outcome would be? You knew Your outcome and still came. I wouldn't have come. I would have asked to be put back inside. Seal the opening shut and let me rot in there. But You still stepped out of the womb and allowed the breath of life to be breathed into You knowing all You would face, which in no way can even be compared to my penance of pain. I celebrate You today, Jesus. All I have is my faith to give back to You. But You have it. You have my heart and my faith, as fractured as it is, You have that too. Happy birthday. Really glad You showed up.

Day 152

We have an offer. I got the call yesterday that someone has put an offer on our house. My first reaction was a lump in my throat. In this market that has recently turned, I'm shocked. But what I'm feeling is overwhelmed. This is the final closure. This is the final piece. When I turn the key in the door for the last time, nothing holds us anymore. And I'm begging You to help me with this. No, I'm thanking You that You will. You've got me through this entire season with so much grace and peace that I am confident You will get me through whatever else is ahead.

I am confident that when I leave this home, You will have one ready for me. I thank You that it is going to meet every need I have. I thank You that I haven't had to look, but I have trusted that when the time comes, what I need will be waiting.

Day 153

I talked to him today about the sale of the house. He was choked up talking about it. His emotion surprised me since he has been gone from it for seven months now. But I guess it is the same for him, that final tie. And maybe knowing that he was taking care of me in some way gave him a sense of peace.

"I really didn't want this to ever happen."

"Me either," he said.

It's hard, Lord. So, as I begin this fast, I'm going to spend that time packing up things, separating things and getting into the frame of mind of the new place and plan that You have for me. I pray that as I pack and pray, You will lead me into what this next season of my life needs to look like. Thank You for the word You've given me for Sunday. I'm still amazed, Father, how messages, like books, come into Your spirit and then get fleshed out to be shared with people. Thank You for the privilege of sharing Your word with people. And thank You that the certainty of that same word can guide my heart when life is completely uncertain.

I went horseback riding this afternoon. And I was so alive. Scared to death, but loved every minute of it. I picked Dee. Julia asked me over and over if I was sure this was the one I wanted. She just looked so sweet that I thought she would be the perfect choice, but Lord have mercy, I can hardly walk tonight. My bootie hurts like my bootie ain't ever hurt. And I've got to speak on Sunday! At this rate I don't even know if I can walk up the steps. They're liable to have to leave the podium on the floor.

But we had so much fun. Damon and Sarah went with us, and Julia who owns the horses took us on this beautiful trail in Camden. And I took in every piece, every sound and every color. I didn't miss one moment. Granted, Sarah and I had to take a potty break in the woods, but except for that it was the perfect outing. Now to ice my butt!

Day 156

I didn't want to teach this lesson today. To be honest I didn't want to speak at all. But You busted up all of my shame today,

Father. You broke it down and exposed it for what it was . . . arrogant, religious pride. I had battled with You for two weeks about this lesson. Ever since You gave me the passage in 2 Timothy, where Paul is talking about the "good fight." And one of the fights worth fighting that I was led to talk about in this message was fighting for your marriage. So in our dialogue about it this morning in the car ride to the church, You were loving but clear.

"How can I tell people to fight for their marriage when I couldn't keep mine together?"

You don't believe in fighting for marriages anymore?

I didn't expect that one. "Yes, I do, Father. Of course I do. But how can I stand in that pulpit divorced? How can I teach from this place? And to these people that are like family to me?"

Baby girl, you need to know that you were no more worthy to teach My word when you were married than you are now.

And with that, every ounce of my shame, my pride and my debate left. You let me know clearly that it is about nothing I will ever do. It has always been and only will ever be about who *You are* and how gracious You are to love me at all. And I guess I did, Father. I thought holding on to my marriage made me holy in some way. But now with it as nothing but a pile of rubble at my feet, the only thing that has ever made me holy is the fact that You are willing to love me.

So I walked up to the pulpit and delivered Your word. A word I believed, but not a word I would have chosen. When I went back to the pastor's ready room between services, my precious friend Brian looked at me as if he could read my mind. He said, "You know, when we look at you up there, we don't see Denise the divorced woman. We see Denise the woman God loves."

The lump that solidified in the base of my throat could only say a gravelly "thank you." And then I went out and delivered the message yet again.

You love me even with all my stuff, Father. And You love me enough to bust up in the face of my arrogance and obliterate my false religion. My, how much there is to learn about You! How wide is Your net for my stuff, how narrow is my thinking . . .

Day 157

This is the last day of the year that has effectively changed my life forever. It has changed me in so many ways. It has taken me from no longer being married, which is still at times overwhelming and almost impossible to believe. It has entered me into a new world of seeing You in a way I never thought was possible, because You have honestly revealed Yourself in the dark places differently than You do in the good times. No, it's that I can see You differently when my heart is broken because it's more open and desperate. That is the difference. My state. Not Yours. There is no turning with You. You will "push or woo," Ken has told me. This time You have pushed.

But in spite of the great loss of this year, what I have gained has been far greater. I've been reading Amy Grant's book called *Mosaic*. And in it she tells this story about having her and Vince's baby girl, Corrina, baptized and dedicated. She said when Corrina was baptized it made her want to get re-baptized. Almost as if it were washing away her past. All the old stuff. And that Vince wasn't going to do it at first. That was until he saw her face when she came up out of the water. She had wondered if he could see the difference in her. But she knew he had, because immediately he started taking off his shirt to get baptized himself.

That story impacted me. This year has felt like a baptizing of sorts, a washing by You, by Your fire, by my tears, by letting go. Just a washing away of all that has held me in its death grip. And You have so beautifully kept me and held me and cleansed me. I am believing that this next year holds some amazing new adventures for me. I'm glad You're going with me. Because I have found You to be exceptionally real to me this year.

Questions

What are some moments during this journey when you have actually felt alive? If you haven't, how can you get to the bottom of what is keeping your heart held under lock and key? Do you need to get into counseling? Divorce care? A grief group of some kind?

There is a great deal of transition in seasons following loss. Loss could come in the form of changing homes, changing names, changing churches, changing friends. What are some of the changes you have had to face in this season? It is important to realize that there is also great opportunity in seasons like this. What are some opportunities your changes hold for you? And what are some things you actually may need to be freed from?

Sometimes after a deep loss we try to go back and "manage," or "access," if you will, all that we *should* have noticed. But in that discovery we might then try to make it "ammunition" in our next relationship. What are some of the discoveries you have made about your previous relationship? Ask God how to allow you to learn from these discoveries without letting them become a hindrance to your actual healing or to what He may have for you in the future.

For me, a real sense of what I had lost came when no one was there to open the lid to my Sweet Potato Butter. What are some things you have lost? The other thing, however, is that through that I saw how God is the God of our details. Take time to think of some of the detailed ways He has loved you during this season. For me it was a jar opener for hard-to-open lids. What has it been for you? After you recount the details, take some time to thank Him for them.

Homework

Begin an "alive journal." Chronicle it with pictures, magazine clippings, whatever creative tilt you want to put on it. But make it about all of the amazing ways your soul is being allowed to experience being alive. If you are not having moments of being alive, I strongly encourage you to seek out a counselor and/or group to walk with you through this journey. Insights other than your own are imperative during this season. And begin to ask the Father to bring life back into your heart and remove any stubbornness from you that would cause you to miss it. Trust me, if you ask for bread like that, He's not going to give you a stone.

Write down your personal places of shame during this journey. Then take them and get alone with your Father and lay them before Him. While you are there, remember that it is Jesus plus nothing. The only worthiness you have for anything is because He died and allowed you to be. Shame is a companion of divorce and other places of loss. It loves to keep you imprisoned by it. Do not leave this season until you have let shame go. Press in, dig in, but "LET IT GO!"

Prayer

O God, in the course of this busy life, give us times of refreshment and peace; and grant that we may so use our leisure to rebuild our bodies and renew our minds, that our spirits may be opened to the goodness of your creation; through Jesus Christ our Lord. Amen.

THE BOOK OF COMMON PRAYER

MONTH 6

IT DOES GET EASIER
(JANUARY)

Day 158

Writing a new year will take some getting used to. Who would have dreamed we'd ever live to see this year. I was certain You would have come back by now. Prayed it many times at those Sunday evening church services when I knew I had to go back to school on Monday. Boy, I was desperate for You then. Been pretty desperate for You now too . . .

When I got up this morning to let Sophie go outside, the air was perfectly crisp. Not cold. Perfect. I was wrapped up in my comfy robe, and if there had been a place to sit that wasn't covered with dew I would have plopped myself right down and savored every minute of it. The sun is brilliant today. I can't find a cloud. And as I inhaled every ounce of it, I sensed You whisper, *This is how this year is going to be, no clouds . . . just brilliance.*

But you know what, Father? Even with all the clouds of last year, You still made it brilliant. The way You loved me. How alive You are to me. And then to top it off, this morning I came into my room to get my study books to study for a while and found the pen I thought I had lost. It came up missing yesterday, and it made me sick in my gut. I thought that maybe I'd find it when I went to pack for my trip, but I knew there was a huge possibility of it being gone. Me and keys and pens and sunglasses . . . pretty pathetic track record. But there it sat. And all I could do was thank You. And once again You spoke. And I felt that gentle whisper that said, *You've thought a lot was lost, but you're going to find lost things this year. They haven't been lost forever.*

I so believe that, Lord. I so believe that everything You have for me, including a genuine, God-reflected love in a man is waiting for me. There are children waiting for me. There is a deeper, richer life waiting for me. In fact, I have an excitement for what is ahead and gratitude for where I now dwell.

But while I'm waiting for more of the things You have for me, would You make me a real student of Your Word? Make what I study stick. Let my memory hold it and absorb it and keep it in the deep places of my heart. Let Your Word just become alive to me so that I can understand it as a teacher comprehends that which they specialize in. I want to specialize in Your Word, and I want to understand it in its deepest places.

That is my prayer, so that I can impart Your Word with authority and wisdom and truth and accuracy. Make it so this year. Just like You told me when I was scared to go back to writing, You said, *You show up and I'll show up*. I believe You will do the same here. If I study . . . You will meet me there.

Be with me as I start this fast tomorrow. May it be as easy as it was last year. May my mind be sharp and alert and my fellowship with You sweet. May You bring me revelation for my next steps and direction for my path. May You bring divine appointments and lead me in what is ahead. That is my prayer for this new year.

Day 161

Remind me never to start a fast with an eight-hour car ride ahead. The caffeine headache was brutal, but it was the reentry back home that was even harder. I'm sure I've said this before, but it's just so fresh. Coming back home is so difficult, but this time it has felt extremely difficult. Figuring out how to be alone and yet not lonely is something I have yet to master. I know I was that way once before. I know that when I was single I was alone and desiring to get married, but I wasn't lonely. Because that is the only world I had ever known. But when you've been in a marriage, even a difficult one, there is still a loneliness that you are unprepared for. It has been quite unsettling.

I think that being home for so long with my family makes coming back harder. But it has required me to ask myself what this new season will look like for me and whether Franklin is truly where I'm to remain or not. I'm honestly open to whatever You have for me. There are days when I'd love to pack up and move to Charleston. But I have to make sure I'm not simply running away from something but running to something. I also need to make sure that I'm not looking for someone or something to fulfill me.

There are days when I think of this deep loneliness, this darkness that accompanies divorce, and I think there is no way I could ever put myself in a situation to feel this way again. It is so scary. The thought of ever being at this place of loss again scares the heebie-jeebies out of me. It almost makes me have no desire to love again. And I'm still angry, I think. Like right now, I feel this anger inside of me. I wish he would have . . .

Oh! I didn't know all of that was in there! I just had a 15-minute breakdown . . . a screaming-out-my-anger fit. Anger over having to separate our stuff. Anger. Obviously it's still there. Looking at my Christmas tree, knowing we have to separate ornaments and know this isn't how You intended it to be. You intended us to share a marriage and a family for the rest of our lives, but both have to be willing to fight for that.

Sophie climbed on my lap as soon as I started crying. Licking my face, my tears. All I could do was thank You for her. Thank You for the gift that she is to me. What a treasure I don't deserve. Whenever I start thinking about spending my life with someone else, all of this emotion comes to the surface. There are so many things my heart wonders, Father. Questions that fill me with fear; questions that fill me with what ifs; questions that fill me with anger. And then all I can do is come back and fall into Your Word. That You will give me the desires of my heart. As my heart seeks after You, I don't have to worry about the what ifs or what should have beens or what could have beens; I can just trust that You know the deepest and most secret places of my heart. Because You placed them there. And it is You I choose to trust. I trust that You will help me continue to get rid of this anger, continue to flush out what needs to go, and I will trust You with my heart in every way. In the words of Peter, "Where else could I go?"

Day 162

I felt You ask me to fast something else. But this time it isn't for 21 days; this time it is for a year. You've asked me to fast buying any clothes this year. I have no idea what that is about, but okay. Whatever You want to show me in this, I'll let You show me . . .

Day 164

The pain won't seem to yield. Both Saturday and Sunday were so hard. I think it is knowing that I am going to have to leave my home combined with the spiritual attack because of this fast. Selling the house has felt far more traumatic than I expected. After I fell apart on Friday, he called me to tell me that we needed to figure out a time to clean out the attic and separate our stuff. I told him I just needed to do it all at once. That it was too hard to think about making it some long, drawn-out process. I just needed to do it and get it over with. Then I had a breakdown in the car and called Packer and asked her if she would come over and help me take down my Christmas decorations.

And what did she come with? She came with a Coke. I'm in the middle of this fast and she comes in with a Coke and a smile. And in the beauty of that moment with my precious friend, I hear You say, *You didn't go after it, but I want you to have it.* So I enjoyed every minute of it. And I was so grateful for her presence. While she was there, the lady who is buying the house came over to measure some of the rooms to see how her stuff would fit. And for a brief moment it looked like hesitation in her eyes. It was almost as if she felt overwhelmed.

She said, "I can't imagine how my stuff will look in here."

I said, "You just have to make it your own. This is how we decorated it. But you decorate it the way you and your family are comfortable."

When she left, I told Packer, "She's liable to back out. Did you see her face?"

"Yes, she looked overwhelmed."

"I know. That's what I saw."

I don't know what it all means. What I do know is that yesterday afternoon while I was spending some time with You, I began looking in my dining room and then I came into my bedroom and began grieving all over again. This really has been a dream home to me. My favorite home we've ever lived in, and that's saying something after five homes and three apartments in 13 years. And even though it still feels unfinished and at times slightly cold to me, it is mine. And it was supposed to be ours for years and years to have children in and to walk in and grow in and live in.

I ended up in a heap again on the bedroom floor, and Sophie came, just like she did on Friday, nuzzling her head right next to mine. What a gift You've given me in her, Father. What a gift You've given me. Even to the point that You knew I needed Chloe to be gone because she was so draining, so You took her for my sake and for hers. She no longer had to suffer, and I didn't have to bear the weight of her middle of the night seizures. And then on top of that You knew what I needed. You knew I needed this bundle of life to make me get up and to make me smile.

During this season of uncertainty and uprooting I am certain that You are walking before me with a sickle, removing the brush and the weeds and preparing the soil for me and my heart. You are moving on my behalf, and I am grateful. Becoming divorced . . . just another piece of the journey.

Day 167

I was half dreading, half looking forward to my meeting with Ken today. I really didn't feel like going, because I knew where we would have to go to get through what I have been feeling this week. And when I went in there I thought, *He'll never know I've had a bad week,* because I was laughing and bubbly when I walked in. As soon as we finished our hellos, he was like, "You seem a little . . . " I don't even remember the word he used because I was too amazed that he could discern my heart so quickly. Honestly, I've met very few people who are as discerning as Ken Edwards.

So I just began to share with him how I had felt that heaviness since I got home. And he, as he so graciously does, began to unravel it with me.

"Do you feel like you're stuck?"

"No, just kind of under it. There are moments when it lifts, but this time it just feels different." That was when I started to weep. I couldn't quit crying.

And, as if he knew exactly what my heart was so scared of, he said, "You're not going to stay here."

And I cried harder. Because I know this in my head, but when you're in the middle of it, sometimes it doesn't feel like you will ever come out of it.

"This lack of place really bothers you."

"Yeah, not having completely settled on a church freaks me out."

He leaned back and crossed his right leg on top of the other. "You know, it's okay to not know where you're going to be right now. I believe God really wants to strip your gears. So, I'm asking you to just flush all you know about church away. Just flush it away. And then just say, 'Lord, here I am', and then see what He brings back to you that He wants you to have for this season of your life. And you know what? It may look different than it's looked before, or it may look very similar. But let Him tell you what He wants for you."

"I think it's really all about being out of control," I said.

"I know that. That's what I've wanted you to see."

"But I know I'm not in control. But I'm losing everything that was mine."

He leaned in and handed me another tissue. "And that's a really hard place to be."

And it is . . . it so is.

Then he asked me, "Did you know at an early age that there was a special call on you?"

And that struck me at my core. Because I had just read a similar statement in my T. D. Jakes devotional yesterday and when I read it I knew that I did know at an early age that God had a plan on my life. "Yes, I did."

"When my wife and I were expecting, she went through a stage where you're real excited, then you're just in this no-man's land, and then you come to the last four weeks and she was like, 'I've got to get this out of me,' and it was half-panic, half-excitement. But she knew she had to get it out. And it came and was delivered. I feel like you're in that final four-week push of your grief and of this divorce."

My face must have registered another layer of fear.

"I'm not saying it will last four weeks, but just that it needs to be over and that when it is gone you are going to deliver something great, because God has something great for you."

"I know that." And I do. Then I added, "I just have to push past this stigma."

That moved him to the edge of his seat. I've never seen him quite like I did in that moment. He said, "I'm going to try not to sound harsh, but you've just got to get over that. I don't see you as divorced. I see you as a beautiful woman who has such a heart for God. And this was not your fault. You did not have a choice in this divorce. And what I see in you in no way has that stigma attached to it . . . and you've got to get rid of that."

I heard him. I heard him clearly. And I do. I have to. Because just the other day, at lunch with a friend, I felt as if I had nothing to offer her because I was divorced.

"You are not seen that way, Denise. That stigma is not on you, and you need to flush that away with the other religious things you've been taught through the years. God does not see you that way. He is hurt that it happened, but He doesn't see you that way, and I'm going to ask you that next time you're in a situation and that wants to come up, ask yourself, 'Where is God with me right now in this moment, and how does He feel about me?'"

I remembered Brian's words to me back in Camden: "When I look at you, I don't see a divorced woman. I just see Denise, a woman of God."

Ken was saying the same thing to me. But today he said it in an even more authoritative way than he had ever said anything to me:

"I want you to receive this from me as the voice of the Lord to you, as one in spiritual leadership over you during this season, that this is not a cloak you are to wear; you are to throw it off of you."

As I got in the car I began to pray immediately, asking You to take all of this from me. Take all of this shame and saturate me with a picture of how You see me. There is so much left to be stripped away, Father. Give me a heart that is free and clean before You. Help me rid myself of these old mindsets and old wineskins and this badge of shame. Remove my shame. Remove this heaviness from me. Just remove it and make me all that You desire to make me.

Day 168

The buyers walked. I had a feeling when I saw that look on her face a few days ago that she would try to use something to get them out of it. There was an issue with the shower that would have been an easy fix; but instead of allowing us to fix it they decided to walk away from the house. As I'm walking out this fast I am confident that You are in every detail, including this one. I don't know what it all means, but what I do know is that I trust You in the middle of it.

Day 171

It's amazing what my conversation with Ken did for me on Thursday. Then Friday night, when I was with Deneen, she reminded me of what I felt You say to me regarding the changes of the seasons. You are speaking, Lord. And yesterday when I went back to my old church, it felt strange. There is a piece of me that is hurt that my pastor has not contacted me through this journey. But I don't want to make any decision based on offense. I want to go or stay based on what You speak to my heart. And I trust You with that. I trust You with my heart.

And since I'm trusting You with my heart, let's just be honest . . . yesterday was another difficult day regarding my "lovey" situation. I thought it was something that was worse every other month, but apparently it is something that I'm going to have to deal with every month. Not bad in the long run of my life, grateful I still have these feelings, not so good for the short run. But still so grateful to You that my body can feel this way.

Another thing I'm noticing is that the possible sale of my home has done something for me. It has increased my desire to have it sold. It really is a lot of house for me. And so hard to create that homey feeling my heart so desperately craves. If I knew this was going to be my house forever, I would pour my heart and soul into it, but I don't know that it will be. And I also know that it is a point of connectedness that ultimately needs to be severed. I also know that there is a plan in the delay. And I am trusting You for provision in every way—from a buyer in Your perfect time, to the money that I will need to live on. Thank You that You are continually trustworthy and available to me. And that You will meet all of my needs.

Day 171

I'm beginning to really see a lot of what You are desiring to accomplish in me through this fast. This is a season of releasing yet again for me. I've already released my marriage, my money, my career; now You are asking me to release those things that would hold my heart in bondage—my shame . . . my legalism . . . my doubts . . .

Legalism has consumed me. And this is where I feel You pressing today. I'm not sure to a complete degree what part it played in my marriage, but I know it was there. I put so much pressure on him to have a relationship with You the way I did. Not realizing that You love each of us uniquely and individually. Even though his choices weren't my fault, I created a beautifully painful environment of judgment.

He and I had to talk this morning. He was anxious over the loss of the sale of the house. And as we talked, today I apologized to him for how I had tried to make his relationship with the Lord look like my own. He thanked me and heard me. But it wasn't for him, honestly. It was for me. In order to truly heal my own heart, I have to be willing to see and admit the areas in which I was wrong. The places in my heart that were fractured and broken and disobedient. I'm sure You'll show me more. And when You do, I may simply repent to You. But today I needed to apologize to him. My only prayer is that through it You will reveal Yourself to both of us in an even greater way.

Day 175

I arrived in Jefferson, Texas, yesterday for Girlfriends' Weekend with my precious friend Kathy Patrick and her wonderful "book club" ladies. I am bunking with Miss Joyce again, who I stayed with when I came for the Books Alive festival back in November, and my precious friend River Jordan is going to be in tomorrow to spend the rest of the weekend with us.

Last night we headed over to a beautiful bed and breakfast where they had amazing hors d'oeuvres for us, and all of the writers that are here this weekend introduced themselves. Afterwards, we went over to the theater for dinner, and I sat by Heather, who I had met back in November. We have talked quite a few times over the past few months, but tonight she asked me when I would be ready to date. I think I broke out in a sweat right there.

"Not now," was the best I could come up with.

It didn't deter her much. "Well, I have a doctor in Nashville that I really want you to meet, so tell me when you're ready." She added shortly after, "He's hot!"

On Friday at lunch she got even more persistent. "I call him Matthew," she said as she proceeded to tell me the rest of his story. He is divorced; she wants to come see me in February and just wants me to let him take us out to dinner. There will be no pressure on either one of us. Then right after she gets through telling me this, her phone rings, and it's him. He has a patient he wants her to call and encourage. And then I hear her say, "I'm here with her now."

Obviously, they have been talking about me.

She said, "Yeah, I'm coming to Nashville so we can all go out to dinner."

When she hung up, I said, "I guess you two have already been talking about me."

"Yes, I've told him all about you," she said with a sly smile.

Day 176

Tonight was the Girlfriend's weekend annual Hair Ball! What a blast we had. This year's theme was sixties night, and my "girlfriends" from Houston hooked me up! They had an extra dress for me that looked like something Goldie Hawn would wear when she was on *Laugh-In*. They dolled up my hair and slapped enough blue eye shadow on me to buy out Rite-Aid. I don't think my hair was that high when I competed in pageants in the '80s! But we danced, and danced and danced, and I heard myself laugh from the bottom of my toes all over again. And it felt wonderful and alive.

When I finally sat back down, Heather grabbed me again because I had yet to tell her if I would be willing to go to dinner with her and Matthew if she came to town. She pulled me toward her and looked at me and said, "Denise, I trust very few people. But from the moment I met you, I knew I could trust you. And Matthew is one of the most precious people I know. Just like you. You two have the same spirit. And I don't know what you've been through, but I know that you deserve someone who will treat you the way you deserve to be treated, and he is that kind of person. You might just end up wonderful friends, but please, at least go have dinner with us and just see what happens."

The time that passed between her last word and my answer felt like an eternity. But I finally said yes. But it brought up so many emotions. I'm afraid. No, petrified. So, when I got back to Miss Joyce's, I climbed back in her chair with her so we could rock. She said, "Baby, don't let fear keep you from loving again." And it would only be fear. It wouldn't be for a lack of desire to be loved or to love someone. I know You have a plan. I know You have a man. I'm not worried about either. I say that with all honesty, Father. But right now it just feels like I'm enjoying learning to be alive.

Day 178

I finished my fast today. This fast was very different from the one we did last year. Last year my entire family each did it in some way and the truths You gave me during that fast were instrumental in walking out last year. This year though the journey was different. This year Your messages to me have been about stripping the old stuff. Piece by piece, layer by layer, ideal by ideal, I'm letting them go. I'm letting them go . . .

Day 179

I was driving to South Carolina for a book event at Kiawah Island this weekend, and I was having my prayer time with my Tony Miller prayer CD. As I was listening to it there was just a sweet moment of worship. I began to think back to the word from Paul Godava that he spoke over me at Joy Springs about how in one day all of the prayers would accumulate and there would be a lifting of the heaviness of this grief in an instant. And even Ken's words to me the other day about how he senses in his heart that I am in that final push of grief and this will be over. A very confirming word.

And so, I'm asking and believing, Father, that next Sunday will be the day. Let it be the day when that final lifting occurs and the real heavy state of grieving will be gone. I'm going to be with my friend Lawana, and I'm going with her to Jentezen Franklin's church, Free Chapel, that day where they will have their prayer and praise service to end their 21-day fast; and I'm just believing that in those moments You will lift this weight.

You know, there has been forward motion. I saw him last week and talked to him yesterday, and I can sense a healing coming even there. I don't miss him the way my heart did a few months back. I pray for him, desire the best for him, but don't ache for him. The loneliness can get overwhelming, but it no longer feels like a loneliness for him.

I think that grieving the way I did over thinking I was going to have to move was also a gift for me. It allowed me to walk through that grief so that whenever I do move there will be a sense of excitement as I pack up my home. I also trust that Your plan for me is so perfect that there is a reason for this delay. I don't know what it is. Joan is convinced this house is a gift to me until You move me to my final home with my new family. Could be. Could be that somehow You are going to give me the resources to keep it for myself. Or could be I just don't need everything in my life gone in this one moment. But whatever it is, I choose to trust You in the middle of it. And I have an excitement knowing You are in the middle of it.

I also felt a real sense of excitement and expectation regarding where You are taking me and my gifts. I have a sense of open doors this year, of divine appointments regarding the words You have given me and how You are calling me to minister to Your people. Doors that only You can open. Thank You for this sweet time I've had with You today. The beauty of fasts is how they draw us in to You to a sweet place of communion. I treasure these times, Father. And I treasure You.

Day 184

You answered my prayer! Not in the way I thought. I honestly expected during that service yesterday for this grief to be supernaturally lifted. But it didn't happen there. But what I did feel in my heart was that this was the day. I even asked other people to pray with me that this would be the day that I would finally be free from this heavy grief. And it was. But not like I thought.

The service was beautiful, and Pastor Franklin delivered this powerful word called "God Wrestlers." I wept through the entire service, and the thing that ministered to me the most was, "Things have been on hold waiting for you to get to this moment." Things were left on hold until Jacob's moment of wrestling with God. I feel like this has been that kind of season for me. I feel like we have wrestled through a lot of things: my fears, my faith and my failures. And I have truly sensed that things have been on hold in my life to get me to this moment. I remember early on after my divorce that Deneen said she believed that You had placed things on hold for me, things that couldn't come to fruition where I was.

The other thing he talked about was that Jacob forever favored that leg. And I have found a new place of favoring in this experience, Father. I favor Your presence now in a way I never have. I favor Your voice. I favor Your desires for me more than my own. I favor You in a way I never have before. The entire church went down for prayer, and I went as well; but there was no supernatural moment. Yet, I still felt in my heart that this was my day. And that if it didn't come with some "supernatural" feeling, I would just trust it by faith.

But on the way home, I knew. I was listening to my praise and worship CD by Free Chapel, Pastor Franklin's church, and I just began to worship You and pour out my heart in a different way. I'm not sure how I cried to the extent that I did and was still able to drive, and sometimes I was crying and laughing at the same time. But I sensed You speaking to me what You spoke to me over 10 years ago at my first Joy Springs. *I have brought you here to restore your joy.* And that is what I felt, Father. Just this sense of pure joy.

I sang at the top of my lungs, *"I'm not moving back, I'm moving ahead. I'm here to declare to you the past is over. In you all things are made new, surrender your life to Christ and we're moving . . . moving forward."* And in those moments I know that You supernaturally lifted my grief. I don't believe I will ever go back to that deep place of grief again. There may be tears, but there will no longer be those desperate, broken places. That place of me is over. And I thank You for that. And I walk that out in faith.

My mom called at some point, but I was too engrossed in worshiping You to answer. By the time I finally got her, my voice was completely gone. I had sung so much there was nothing left. She got a kick out of that, but I told her what You had done. And as I lay my head down tonight, I thank You again. I thank You that not one word from You or one promise for my life will fall to the ground. You will perform each one. And today . . . this was the one You chose.

My T. D. Jakes devotional said this today: "There is no way you can plan for the future and dwell in the past at the same time. I feel an earthquake coming into your prison! It is midnight—the turning point of days! It is your time for a change. Praise God and escape out of the dungeons of your past. And at midnight Paul and Silas prayed and sang praises unto God: and the prisoners heard them. And suddenly there was a great earthquake, so that the foundations of the prison were shaken: and immediately all the doors were opened and everyone's bands were loosed (Acts 16:25-26)."[1]

You broke me free from my prison today, Father. And You did it with my praise . . . You did it with my praise.

Day 186

When I woke up this morning there was such a sense of Your presence, and it just set the tone for my heart today. I thought of him. I love him. I believe I will always love him in some way. But I know it wasn't the kind of love You created for a husband and a wife. I believe You have something deeper, richer, more honest and real. A God-like love, even though I know we're all human. But I don't miss what we had. And for the first time this morning, I didn't "miss" him.

And this was a completely different reentry back home. All the rest have been painful and hard. But this one . . . this one comes with expectation. Expectation of the future You have for me. The "new place" You will one day take me. And the "new season" You are establishing me in.

In my session with Ken today we got back on the subject of church. He shared with me a song about "fishin' " and how it takes "good bait," and we talked about the whole concept of what "good bait" actually is. As we processed church, I had this lightbulb moment of why I've been so attracted to The Journey. I think it is the pastor's transparency. He can say some things sometimes that make me cringe, like the first time he said "crap" from the pulpit. Granted, I say crap, too, and on some days more colorful words, I do have two Shih Tzus mind you, but I am amazed at his heart and the realness with us as a church. I don't think I've ever known that kind of transparency in the pulpit before. And in a season like this, my heart craves it. And I think that is why I weep every time he preaches.

And maybe this is just a different season for me. I know what I needed in my previous season I found in the church where I was going. But for whatever reason it seems to no longer be my home. I love the people. But the church is just no longer my home. I love the worship, but my heart doesn't belong there anymore. Can I clearly say The Journey is home? No, but what I can say today is that Jamie's messages connect with my heart in a real and genuine way.

Then Ken and I talked about my own story. "How do I share what I've been through without it identifying me?" I asked him.

"Denise, it is transparency that breaks other people's yokes. You share the pieces that are yours."

"But this is his story."

"Not all of it. You were in the middle of this story. And you have made decisions during this story that have affected your heart and your healing. And it is okay to share your part of this story. And because of what you have gone through and your willing-ness to share it, people will be delivered from their own places of bondage and brokenness."

"You know . . ." I said, remembering, "there have been moments that I've taught when I have shared this story about when I was on a research trip in Savannah for my second Savannah book. It was the first time I realized I could have an affair and no one would know. And the attack on me that came with just that one thought of the possibility that infidelity actually existed for me had me watching the Food Network all weekend and boycotting Barry Manilow on my iPod."

He laughed.

"But that made me real to those ladies. Some of them will still quote that story to me. It just resonated with them in such a deep way. And all I was doing was telling my story. I can't change it. I can't change my story, Ken. It is a part of who I am, and I believe it has shaped the calling God has given me."

"I believe you're exactly right. And it is okay to share your story."

"You know, I felt the Lord tell me in the beginning of this jour-ney that if I honored my former husband, He would honor me."

"I believe you have, and I believe He has."

"Me too. And now I have to discover how I continue to honor him by sharing where I've walked in this journey."

"I am confident you will find that place."

So, Father, I just thank You tonight for that conversation. Thank You for showing me that my wounds are here for a reason. And that it's okay to lay them bare so that others' wounds can be healed. You are a healing, Jesus, and You are faithful to heal all of our diseases, even the ones of our soul. Thank You that You are healing mine . . .

Day 187

When did my heart start to shut down? I can't help but ask that question. How can I not ask it when my heart has come back alive? In order to "come back alive" it had to have once been alive. And it was. I know it was, because I've spent the last 15 years saying, "My college years were the best years of my life." And every time those words would come out of my mouth I would think, *What does that say about this season? Shouldn't the season you are in always be the "best season of your life"?* Yet in the living out of my marriage, this was always my response.

I believe it happened incrementally. It happened after I first moved here and the dream of music disappeared, and then slowly the relationships and experiences that I allowed into my life brought pain and heartache. And that was when I allowed the inferiority and insecurity to settle over my soul and, piece by piece, I gave a piece of my heart away.

Because that is what has to happen, Father. We have to give it away. No one can take it from us. And I could have claimed it. Grabbed it back and refused to let it go. But I handed it over piece by piece, and in doing that, I denied the God that You are. Forgive me, Father, for handing over my heart, the very thing You asked me to protect, the very thing You asked me to love You with first and foremost. I handed it over to a far lesser god. And in doing that, I lost myself, the God-given design that You had created for me. You had created this thriving, vibrant, alive soul. And I became a hollowed-out shell of a being to whom You, in Your mercy, gave glimpses of life when You would let me teach or write a story about a feisty, say-whatever-she-wants-to-say young heroine named Savannah.

I should have claimed this piece of me back inside of my marriage. It shouldn't have had to come back through a divorce. I should have looked into the face of everything that was wrong and broken and refused my heart to be snatched away, the heart You designed, the heart You created. But I can't go back, Father. I can only go forward. I can only trust that You will write into my story all of the broken places and weave something redeemable. And I believe You have.

So, as we claim back my heart, there will be more crazy jaunts down Main Street at Disney World, pushing a woman in a wheelchair with two new hips. There will be snow angels and singing in the car at the top of my lungs. There will be more belly laughs and dinners with good friends and being willing to push my broccoli to the side of the plate if I want to, or to eat every last bite if I want to do that too. But all I know is that never again will I hand my heart over to be shut down. I have claimed it back, Father. And just as I gave it piece by piece, I am claiming it back piece by piece.

Again, forgive me. Forgive me for allowing my maneuvering and self-protection and lack of faith in You to cause me to miss some places You were moving in my heart. I, in essence, was saying that the sacrifice You made for me on the cross wasn't enough. That You weren't worthy enough to be trusted. I know so much better now, Father. I can trust You with anything. And I do. I trust You with every piece of my heart . . . and my soul . . . and my mind . . . and my strength.

Questions

What is reentry like for you? What is it like when you've gone away for an evening? Or gone away for a weekend and you come back home to the quiet of your house or to the different dynamic that the absence of a partner brings? What does that look like for you?

Divorce holds a lot of different heartaches that death doesn't. One of them is the dividing of property. What did the process of dividing your property look like? Is there anger or bitterness over what you've lost that you need to ask the Lord to remove so you can get on to living the "abundant life" He has for you? If so, get honest. Invite Him into the pain of it and then release it. Whether you take something to Goodwill, toss it in the trash or sever it in your soul, let it go.

What shame do you still hold on to regarding your divorce? What guilt has tried to consume you? Let it go. Release it. Hand it over to the Father and ask Him to give you a picture of how He sees you. And then ask yourself, *Who am I allowing to shepherd my heart during this season?*

What religious or judgmental attitudes have you had about people who were divorced? What has your own experience shown you in how God sees people's hearts? Ask trusted friends what patterns they may see. Be careful to look at it through the lens of His Word. We can swing that pendulum too far to any side. That is why we need to try our best to see hearts the way He does.

Homework

Take this month to really focus on praising God. I know how hard that can be when you feel like you are in the thick of things that don't feel like they have anything worth praising God for. But praise does something powerful. Isaiah 61:3 tells us to put on the garment of praise for the spirit of heaviness. Praise removes heaviness. So, try this month to fast something. It doesn't have to be food; maybe it is noise in the car or television in the morning or at night. And spend that time listening to praise and worship music and singing those songs of praise to Him.

Also, take some time this month to remember. Remember when you began to give your heart away and allow it to be shut down. Was it specific experiences, specific people, specific moments? Write them down and then spend some time in earnest repentance, breaking any agreements you have made with the enemy to believe that "God isn't enough" or "God isn't capable," and surrender to Him your full heart. Claim it back from the "lesser gods" you've given it over to and allow Him to begin to bring back the alive heart He created for you to have.

Prayer

Lord, make us instruments of your peace. Where there is hatred, let us sow love; where there is injury, pardon; where there is discord, union; where there is doubt, faith; where

*there is despair, hope; where there is darkness, light; where
there is sadness, joy. Grant that we may not so much seek to
be consoled as to console; to be understood as to understand;
to be loved as to love. For it is in giving that we receive; it is
in pardoning that we are pardoned; and it is in dying that we
are born to eternal life. Amen.*

ATTRIBUTED TO ST. FRANCIS OF ASSISI
THE BOOK OF COMMON PRAYER

Note

1. T. D. Jakes, *Hope for Every Moment: 365 Days to Healing, Blessing and Freedom* (Shippensburg, PA: Destiny Image, 2007).

MONTH 7

CHANGING PATTERNS
OF BEHAVIOR

(FEBRUARY)

Day 193

Can you drown from an IV? Seriously, I'm not that big, and when I was lying in the ER yesterday, and two bags of IV fluids were pouring into my body, I asked Damon and Valencia if I could drown. They got a real kick out of that. Fortunately by then I could actually get a kick out of something myself. If I hadn't been so weak earlier I would have gotten a kick out of Damon rushing out of the room when I asked for the pan to throw up in because the admitting lady typed slower than Christmas. I'm saying that if I hadn't been so sick I would have pushed the lady out of the way and typed my own name. I was so sick I thought I was going to have to crawl out of the wheelchair and lay on the dirty hospital floor before she could finish my telephone number.

Finally, she rolled me into my room in the ER, and I was barely able to drape my body across the hospital bed. I'm lying there with half of my body hanging off of the bed, my eyes half shut, and the ER doctor, who looked nothing like George Clooney, mind you, started asking me questions. I felt like Tom Hanks on *Castaway* with some absurd doctor asking him to give an account of the plane crash when all the man wants is some water, food and clean underwear. Honestly, if I had had the strength to raise my hand there was a huge potential I would have flipped him off. But I could barely raise my right eyebrow. So, I mumbled something, and finally a nurse came in and helped me get on the cot, and I heard him say something about IVs, and the next thing I know my eyes are finally back open and I'm wondering if they are trying to drown me.

When Damon finally got me home and back in bed, I was feeling a thousand percent better. I had a stomach bug, courtesy of a group of fifth-graders, that I had had since I'd gotten home Friday; and by the wee hours of Sunday morning, I could feel my body completely shutting down. I had no idea I was so dehydrated, but obviously I was, because enough fluid to drown small farm animals brought me back to life.

As I'm lying here today recuperating, I'm struck by the fact that being sick hasn't thrown me back into a place of grief. Which gives me another glimpse of how You truly touched my heart on my trip home last week. Thank You, Father, that in the midst of even a stomach bug You see me. That I am healing. And maybe I needed a little bit of time to rest. So I'll take it. I'll take this time with You. Even if it's lying here in my bed. I'll take it.

Day 195

Here's what my T. D. Jakes devotion said today:

A terrible thing happens to people who give up too easily. It is called *regret*. It is the nagging, gnawing feeling that says, "If I had tried harder, I could have succeeded." When counseling married couples, I always encourage them to be sure they have done everything within their power to build a successful marriage. It is terrible to lie down at night thinking, "I wonder what would have happened if I had tried this or that." Granted, we all experience some degree of failure. That is how we learn and grow . . . The problem isn't failure; it is when we fail and question if it was our lack of commitment that allowed us to forfeit an opportunity to turn the test into a triumph. We can never be sure of the answer unless we rally our talents, muster our courage, and focus our strength to achieve a goal. If we don't have the passion to be relentless, then we should leave it alone.[1]

Father, I don't know a lot of things, but I know I was relentless in the pursuit of a whole marriage. I know that even at the end, with the incredible broken state of where we were, if there would have been any lifeline to grab hold of, I would have grabbed hold. But I was able to walk away knowing I had done everything I could humanly do. Yet, at the end of the day, even that would not have given me the freedom to be here. The only one who could truly release me is You.

I have had people ask me, "How do you know it is okay to leave your marriage?" I tell them the only thing I know to tell them: "People will release you from your commitments every day. But only God can release you from a covenant." And that is what marriage is. A covenant. Father, I am so grateful for the one piece I have not had to experience through this, and that is regret in wondering if there was something else I could have done. Had I done enough? Was there another stone to turn over? And I am grateful that even if all of my friends and family would have released me, even if he had released me, I would only release myself when I knew You had said, "This far and no farther."

Day 197

Heather came in this evening. The girl I met in Jefferson in November. She had been wanting to come and spend some time with me, so we chose this weekend. I told her I had been really sick, but she was comfortable with spending time on the sofa and just hanging out and enjoying each other's company. When she got here we picked us up a pizza for dinner and sat on the sofa and watched a movie she had brought with her and just enjoyed each other's company. She did tell me that she had told her friend Matthew that we could have dinner this weekend. And that was when I told her, "I just don't think I'm ready. I don't think I want to date anyone while I'm still in this house. It just feels weird going out with someone and still being in this house that I've lived in with him, and bringing someone to this home. I just don't think I'm ready yet."

There was no debate. She took my answer and simply accepted it. Sweetly and without question. I was so grateful. I'm not sure whether my response was right or not, but the thought created so much anxiety that it was the only response I felt like I could give in that moment. So, once again, Father, I'm trusting You with my heart.

Day 198

I went and picked us up some McDonald's for breakfast. Perfect way to help my stomach heal, right? While we were sitting in the kitchen talking, Matthew called. She acted like I wasn't in the room. I had officially reverted to sixth-grade behavior. But she graciously told him I simply wasn't ready to date. That I really wanted to get my house sold and this process of my life settled and not bring anyone into the middle of that. Honestly, it had all just felt awkward. And for me it felt too soon. For my heart. And I'm scared. Still so unsure. Even though I've prayed and asked You to protect me.

And You have protected me. I've watched You already protect me. And Heather is protecting me here, but I'm protecting me too. I was the one who pushed the pause button. Heather would have had him come over immediately, but I pushed the pause. I process everything. I mean, I'm thinking I need to solve all the world's problems on a first date. What is his stance on children, discipline, Typhoid fever?! It's crazy. I am going to have to learn to turn my brain off and realize that there are things about people that have to be discovered. Pulled out. Unearthed, if you will. And those are the things you don't have to know immediately, which is part of the joy of the discovery process. I can't believe I just called the discovery process a joy . . . My word, I'm healing.

And I believe there is a huge piece of me that hasn't wanted to date. I've simply wanted to meet that person and him be Your man. Because I go back to what I believe You spoke to my heart: "I will get my man to you." So, if that is true, then I trust that.

My confidence is in that. There is fear to push past; it is inevitable
because of where I come from. I don't want to get hurt. I don't
ever want to hurt again. But no matter who I meet there will be
pain. It may look different than what I've thought, but humans
hurt. It is a state of our fallenness.

I know I've done the harder things in life, Father. I know I have.
Leaving my marriage was the hardest thing I've ever done. Staying
in my marriage was hard as well. Staying pure in the confines of
that marriage was difficult too. But can I trust me? That is where
the doubt comes in. I have no doubt in You, Father. My only doubt
is me. I hate this! It totally freaks me out and totally excites me at
the same time. I never wanted to be here. How many times through
the years have I said, "I'm so glad I don't ever have to date again."
And here I am. Here I am . . .

Day 200

I woke up totally freaked out today in my prayer time. So
we had a very open and honest conversation regarding my feelings
about dating and going out with Matthew. What I felt in my heart
and heard today as I prayed was *quit obsessing and live*. Oh my, do I
ever obsess over everything. I really do. And I realize it goes back to
my "maneuvering." My trying to manage life instead of live life. A
tormented thoughtfulness, if you will.

But I felt You say, *It is okay to just enjoy something. Quit making
such a big deal out of it and enjoy whatever life offers you.*

So I called Deneen, because I needed to hear what she had to
say. She pretty much cut to the chase: "You need to quit looking
at this as a husband. You need to look at this as just a date. As a
step of healing. As one more piece in the puzzle that you need to
do. The likelihood of him being the one is slim anyway. But you
need to not let the house or him hold you anymore."

It was a real confirmation to what You had spoken to me.
Then she said, "Why don't you call Ken?"

So I did, which I never do outside of our office time together.
I left him a message so long that the answering machine ran out.

So I called Mom, and she agreed. "Just go, baby. There is no harm in that."

Ken called in a few minutes, and he immediately started, "Before you say anything, how do you feel? What's your initial feeling?"

I paused. "I want to go." And I did. I really did. I was just scared, scared to move in that moment, let alone to date.

"Then go."

"But I'm scared."

"You're going to be scared. This is a scary thing."

"I just feel like it is too soon. Like I should wait longer even though I know there is no timetable to grief."

"Would you know if you went out with him if it was too soon?"

That made sense. "Yes, I would . . . ooh, that's good. I hadn't though of that."

He laughed. "I know, that's why you called me."

"Yes, that's why I pay you the big bucks," I said. "But I'm such an over-processor."

"You think? I heard your message, remember."

I laughed. "I've spent the last 13 years having to figure out where this action or that action was going to lead us and not feeling like I could simply enjoy a moment. And so this morning I was praying when I felt like the Lord said, *It's okay to enjoy moments. Just enjoy this moment. Don't overanalyze it.*"

"Okay, so that's your homework assignment. Go out on a date and don't process it. Just enjoy it."

The expletive flew. I couldn't help it. It was the only thing fitting.

He howled on the other end. "Just don't give your heart away."

"That's the thing about me, Ken. I know me. I give my heart to people."

"I know. But protect your heart. Anyway, he's not coming with a ring."

Then I cracked up.

"He would if he knew what was good for him, but he won't. So just have a good time. And if you change your mind, you don't have to go. Then you can tell me how it went."

"I told Deneen I couldn't go out this weekend because I wasn't going to see you until next Monday. So she told me I just had to call you then."

He laughed. "I like her."

Mark and Deneen called me last night and put me on the speakerphone so I could tell them everything Ken had said. Mark said, "You're discerning enough to know how you feel. You've walked through enough that has made you a woman who knows what she needs, and God will lead you." Simply writing that down gives me confidence.

He also said, "Most doctors don't have a sense of humor, and you'll definitely need someone with a sense of humor!"

You know, Father, I'm not the same woman I used to be. I'm not a cowering woman afraid to lose someone. I am a woman of God. A mighty woman of God, and I can walk in that grace and confidence. I can set the tone with the same kind of confidence I had 15 years ago. And I don't have to be afraid. I can walk away from anyone that I need to. And I can also enjoy living! I can enjoy just living! Becoming divorced . . . just another piece of the journey.

Day 201

I sent an email to Heather this morning. I just didn't have a peace about sending it yesterday after she left. So this morning as I was praying, I asked You once again to guard my heart, and that if I wasn't truly ready to date, You knew that. And for You to protect me, but that I was at least going to be willing to allow the door to open. Which for me is a huge element of claiming my heart back and enjoying life. So, she called me right back. I knew she'd have a heart attack. And she pretty much did.

"Girl, you have given me a heart attack. You're not going to believe what I did. Matthew started in yesterday morning about you immediately when I got to his office. He just didn't understand why you didn't want to meet him, and I got pretty protective of you and told him he just needed to back off, because you weren't ready. And that I didn't know when you would be. I told him that he was going to have to wait for this house to sell. And that you weren't like me, you had a spirit that I needed to protect, and he just needed to back up. And if he didn't want to wait on you, he could just move on; but if he did want to wait on you, then he just needed to wait. He looked so dejected when I finished with him, Denise."

I was sitting upright in my bed. "I'm sure he did."

"He told me that he was going on to Mayo Clinic. He had a conference scheduled to teach at, so he was just going to go up a week early."

"Well, that's okay. Maybe he needed to go on up, and he wouldn't have if I had told you this yesterday. And you know what, if he comes home and doesn't want to ask me out, then that's okay too. The Lord knows even better than me when I'm ready. Who knows . . ." I said laughing. "We might not even be attracted to each other."

"Well, I don't think that's going to happen, but if not, I think you would be wonderful friends to each other."

She said she called him after she got my email and left a message and told him, "I know you're probably mad at me, but if you could call me, I would appreciate it."

We hung up; and you know, Father, I am so at peace. If he thinks it is too much drama, or I'm too flighty, and he doesn't want to call me, that's okay. It will be a little disappointing not to meet him, but I have prayed so hard for You to protect me from anyone that I'm not supposed to meet that I have a perfect confidence in You. You know my heart. You made it, and You are beautifully healing it, and I am trusting completely in You for the area of a new beginning as well. And I know You have my husband picked and planned for me.

You have proven once again that You are so capable of taking care of me. Thank You, though, for reminding me that it is not my responsibility to manage my life. It is my responsibility to hand my heart to You and enjoy the life You have given me, that if I will do that You will take care of the rest. And take care of the rest, You have.

Day 202

This is my last first. It's Valentine's Day. He even called me first thing this morning, but I don't think the significance of today was on either of our radars. It wasn't until I hung up that I remembered. And all I could do is thank You that You would be very present in this Valentine's. My last few Valentine's have been disappointing. I had had expectations of one thing and left wounded and hurt. But not tonight. Tonight I am full because my expectations no longer rest in someone else. But they rest in You.

And what a perfect evening you gave me. My friends Ashley and Tommy and I went to my favorite restaurant, Radius 10, where my favorite chef, who I wrote about in *Savannah by the Sea*, makes his famous shrimp and grits. And we ate like kings and queens. Ashley had fixed my hair all messy and up on the top of my head. I wore my black velvet blazer, black tank and red Baccarat heart necklace. I felt beautiful and alive.

Tommy brought us roses and a card, and I brought them both bags of candy, and for three hours we laughed, talked, ate and shared our lives. And I was so alive. My friends Kim and Lee were there and came over and sat with us for about 30 minutes before they left. And throughout the evening You redeemed another piece of the soul of me. Thank You for friends, for food, for fun and for a day to celebrate people that you love. And thank You for the people that love me.

Before the day ended, I had a conversation with a friend who was telling me about the Valentine's Day card she had bought her husband. She said that she realized there were some Valentine's cards she could never buy because so many cards said things she didn't feel or couldn't say. And I knew. I knew what it was like to stand in front of the Valentine's card section and open up card after card that in no way were representative of where my heart was or what my situation was. And I saw in her situation a glimpse of what my future could have held. And I saw in You today a glimpse of how freeing and life-giving Your love can be.

If I had picked out a card for You today it would simply say this: "In a world of broken people, You remain the one who continually believes broken things are repairable. In a world of pain, You remain the one who continually believes that even painful things can be redeemable. And in a world where a heart needs to know that it is loved, You send reminders every day. And for this heart that has been looking, I've seen them . . . and in seeing them, I've seen You. I love You, Father. Deeply. Passionately. And freely."

Day 203

Lord, thank You that I didn't wake up this morning feeling hurt or frustrated. But I woke up singing. Yep, singing. Even going outside in the cold I loved the feeling of the sun on my face. Thank You that I'm *"Not moving back, I'm moving forward."* And that I was alive and fully present in that moment last night, and that I am going to be alive today, substitute teaching fifth-graders. Even though they about killed me last time. In fact, I'm beginning to wonder if substituting is financially feasible at this point . . .

Today when I was substituting, I was reading my former pastor Dan Scott's book *Naked and Not Ashamed.* The part that really struck me was the section on co-dependency. He talked about when we are operating from a healthy and God-like perspective, Jesus is the outer shell of our lives; then our families, then our friends; and how life is funneled through the outer shell before it can get anywhere else. But in a co-dependent relationship, we allow that individual to become the outer shell, and everything we do funnels through their thoughts and responses. And that this is very different from serving someone and having a heart of service for them.

As I read this, it was so profound to me. I had allowed him to have my inner circle. Almost every prayer I prayed was about him. And when I read this it was as if for the first time I could actually see it. I could visualize what I had allowed to happen to my heart. I don't ever want to forget this, Father. This is a picture that can set hearts free.

Day 207

I'm having more revelations after reading that excerpt from Pastor Dan's book. I'm realizing how I've been so afraid of conflict. I will even push back my thoughts or heart's desire so I won't offend someone else. I don't do this in ministry. Bring something up in ministry that I know is wrong or needs to be dealt with and I deal with it immediately. I believe that is because I feel like there I am defending You, not me. Even though as I'm writing this I'm well aware that You don't need this little petite Southern girl's defense . . . do you . . . ?

But in relationships I have so far to go. Though I will say I had a small moment of victory the other day. A friend pressed one of my buttons the other day at lunch. They were telling someone that I didn't mind spiritually leading the man that I would marry. I had a pretty quick and emphatic response, "I don't want that!" It was a pretty loud response too. There isn't an ounce in me that wants to carry someone along. Watching someone learn something or encounter You in a way they never have before is one thing. But praying someone to become the person they simply need to have the chutzpah to be is something completely different. I don't have the time or energy for that. The man that captures my heart will be a man that is chasing You. If he ain't chasing You, he ain't chasing me!

And there was just this voice that rose up out of me to answer her when normally I might have sat there and just kept my mouth closed, because I didn't want to hurt her feelings. But things, they are a changin' . . .

And then I felt like You allowed me to come to terms with this piece of me in an even greater way. You definitely took me seriously when I said "get out of me whatever got me here." One of my friends who is in a difficult situation right now, and I have really tried to be a friend to during this season, called on Saturday. For the last four months there have been multiple times when she has called and taken her anger out on me. Her tone is harsh and demanding, and it makes me have that shriveled-up-inside feeling. Ken and I talked about it one day, and he said, "Next time she does that, ask her, 'What do you want me to do with that?' "

So, on Saturday, she was talking about her situation again and how bad it was, and it breaks my heart. It really does. But I've done all for her I can do. And her attitude was so angry, and it was all projected at me as if she resented me and the way my journey has been walked out. At one point during the conversation I was trying to help her think of some things she might be able to do to help her situation, and she said, "I didn't call for your opinion. Do you not think I'm doing everything I can?"

That was when I stopped her. "Hey, wait a minute. If you are angry with me over something, then let's talk about what you're really angry about. I'm not trying to do anything but encourage you. If I could change all of this, I would. I would pay your rent if I could. But I can't. I just can't. But we've been friends for a long time, so if you are upset with me, you just need to tell me. Because every time you call you talk to me as if you are mad at me, and I can't understand this if I don't even know what the issue is."

There was complete silence, to the point I thought she had hung up. "Are you there?"

She finally said, "Well, I just won't call you anymore. I've got to go."

"So, you're going to toss our friendship aside without a conversation."

"I've got to go." And she hung up.

It was so sad to me. But I knew that for my own personal healing it was time to set boundaries. I can no longer allow my life to be funneled through fear of someone being upset with me. I simply can't do that anymore. If people get upset with me and even tell the details and personal places of my story, there is nothing I can do. You alone can be my defense. But I believe You were making it clear that there are some patterns of my behavior that have to change for me to walk in a whole mindset. And this is one of them. The dynamics of our relationship were even becoming dysfunctional to a co-dependent level. And I believe it is because of the pain of the seasons we are both walking through. I can't help but believe this is as much about her healing as mine.

Father, be with my friend today. Be with her in her hurting place. Meet every need that she has, and most of all, may her heart seek out true freedom and may she allow friends who truly love her love her like only real friends can . . . teach me to be a friend. A friend who loves well . . .

I met with Ken today and told him about what happened. He said, "This is the pendulum from which everything swings, especially for you. You have to find this freedom."

And I do. And I believe I am.

"Can I tell you something else?" I said.

He laughed. "Sure."

"The other day I was riding through Franklin, thinking, *If I die, who is going to bury me? The pastor I have hardly knows me. Or if I met someone and wanted to get married, who would marry me?* And it was so clear, I just sensed the Lord say, *I gave you Ken to shepherd your heart during this season.*"

He smiled.

"So, thank you. Thank you for shepherding this ridiculously screwed up and desperate heart."

"All I ask is that you keep your heart aware of all the ways your Father is shepherding your heart."

I smiled and raised my right eyebrow. "I am . . . He showed me you."

Day 208

Aunt Alice, or Mervine, as we like to call her, and I headed to Camden today for my dad's sixty-fifth birthday celebration. I picked her up at her home in Murfreesboro, and off we went. As we drove the eight-hour drive home, I had this desire to know my history. So I asked her all kinds of questions about my grandparents and my aunts and uncles.

She told me that my grandmother wouldn't let my granddaddy touch her until they got married. She had said, "He tried to kiss me once, and I pushed him away." Then Mervine shared what she remembered on the day my grandmother died. She died when my dad was only eight years old, from sinus cancer. She had been bedridden for a long time, and when my dad's younger brother George went into her room that day and saw her bed made up, he said, "Woohoo! Where's Mama?" And at four years old they had to tell him that she had gone to heaven.

Mervine remembered dates and moments. She shared with me stories of her siblings that I had never known, of their broken places and her daddy's fractured love. And I held each one in the depths of my heart. I love these people. In my Savannah books, I've tried to use each one of their names, because there is shared history with family that you can't find anywhere else. And for some reason, I needed to know mine.

Day 211

I sent him an email yesterday. I needed to do it for me. I told him how sorry I was for the moments that I had made him feel inadequate. I also told him about my revelation of co-dependency and what that looked like for me, and how I had placed him on the throne of my heart. I don't know if he understands, but I needed him to know that I saw my own stuff. He called today and left me a message, assuring me I had nothing to apologize for. That I had shown grace more than he'd ever known, but that if I needed to do this for my healing, then he understood and accepted it. And this is about healing, Father. And I believe this is another piece of mine.

Questions

What are your greatest fears about entering into a relationship again? Which fears do you feel are projected from your past relationship? Now write down what you feel are healthy concerns as you move forward in relationships.

Our mind can be one of Satan's deadliest weapons against us. He loves to make us "over-processors," as I call it. Or "under-processors" for some. How has God called us to watch over our minds? What tools has He given us regarding our thoughts? What thoughts are you allowing to cause you to miss the "enjoyment" of the life He has for you?

Who are the people during this season who have shepherded your heart? What has God given you through them to help bring healing to you?

Old patterns of behavior are hard to break. Yet, God in His mercy will bring up opportunities for us to identify those old patterns and make the decisions not to repeat them. "It ain't easy," as one woman who used to go to my dad's church said one time. But it is necessary. What are some co-dependent or old ways of behaving that you need to begin breaking the cycle of? Write them down, repent of them, even ask someone for forgiveness regarding them if necessary, but begin to recognize what they look like in your life. When we begin to recognize what the enemy looks like to us, he loses his power.

Homework

Take the time this month to thank those who have shepherded your heart during this season. It will mean so much to them. (I'm Southern and old school—so I don't think there is anything better than a handwritten note.)

This isn't like any homework we've had so far, but I believe this one is essential, for many of you, to your healing. If there are any relationships in your life that are taking on the same patterns of dysfunction that you had in your marriage, it is time to set up boundaries regarding them. Write them down if you need to. Have a conversation with your friend and be willing to step aside from this relationship for a while if you must. But prayerfully ask God what you need to do regarding these relationships in your life.

Prayer

O God, by whom the meek are guided in judgment, and light riseth up in darkness for the godly: Grant us, in all our doubts and uncertainties, the grace to ask what thou wouldest have us to do, that the Spirit of wisdom may save us from all false choices, and that in thy light we may see light, and in thy straight path may not stumble; through Jesus Christ our Lord. Amen.

THE BOOK OF COMMON PRAYER

Note

1. T. D. Jakes, *Hope for Every Moment: 365 Days to Healing, Blessing and Freedom* (Shippensburg, PA: Destiny Image, 2007).

MONTH 8

TRUST . . . WILL YOU OR WON'T YOU

(MARCH)

Day 219

When I got home from South Carolina, I had to fight that old "alone" feeling. It wasn't grief, just loneliness. And I so don't want the enemy to use that against me in any way. I know that could be the one thing to get me into a relationship quickly that might not be right for me. I think that is why You protected me from Matthew. I mean, here was a man who was so anxious to meet me, and yet You graciously protected my heart, and his. Maybe my heart isn't ready yet. Maybe he isn't the one I've prayed for and I could be misguided in some way. But I know that You know. You know what I need and when I need it. And You have protected me so beautifully, and I believe You have honored my asking. Because You so know that my heart meant it. I continually go back to that Scripture from the Sermon on the Mount that says, "Which of you, if his son asks for bread, will give him a stone?" (Matt. 7:9, *NIV*).

And yet it all still amazes me. How You have loved and so protected and provided and been with me during this season. I'm not sure why that amazes me. Maybe because I know I don't deserve it, but You're continually teaching me that as well. That I don't *deserve* anything. But You also remind me that You know my heart. As much as I would have loved to meet Matthew, I want Your will more. I want Your perfect will, with no confusion. I truly only want that one person that You have created for me.

There are still fears I have at times of what You may bring me. But I go back to what happened that evening with me and Cyndi when I had everything that she asked for and could give it to her. I felt as if You said, *Haven't I proven to You that I care not just about*

Your needs but also about Your desires? And I have to trust that means in every part of my life.

I'm at peace, Father, knowing the amazing extent of Your love. And I'm also at peace not wanting to meet someone because I'm lonely, but because I'm ready. *I* knew I was ready the first time around. This time I'm asking that *You* bring him when *You* know I'm ready. Because I trust that You know even better than I do.

Day 222

I recently reconnected with one of my childhood friends. Over dinner we shared our stories. I told her about this journey and how You and I have walked through it. She sent me a precious email the other day that said, "What you didn't say about your divorce spoke so loudly to me." She said she was praying that she would learn how to do that more. Father, that has nothing to do with me. I don't know how I've done it. There are days when allowing the bitterness and anger of all of it to consume me would feel so much easier. But this is only a piece of my story; it isn't the whole of it. And to allow those feelings to stop me from moving forward would be a pitiful way for all of this to end.

Thank You for allowing my heart to remain open and available to You; and I trust You to be my defense. I honestly do. I trust You to guard my heart. And I trust that Your kindness will lead me to repentance in whatever area is needed.

Day 229

It's been a week since I've written anything. The spaces of time are growing wider and wider. If I'm being honest, Father, there are moments when I almost forget I'm even doing this. We talk so much separate from these pages that I forget that I find You here too. But then I remember. The beautiful thing is, there isn't so much in my heart now. There isn't so much consuming me. Maybe this is what they call healing. It was a year ago today that this journey started. I wouldn't have even known that had I not pulled out some of my old journals from when this all began to unfold. But knowing that also reveals where I am and how far I've come.

Spring has arrived. I see it in how daylight hangs around just a little longer. I feel it in the warmth that lingers on my face. I notice it in the sun as it hits my desk and fills up my office with such longed-for light. And it is in the soul of me. I feel it deep inside; and even though it runs so deep; it flows out so free. A new freedom. Not the freedom of being released from my marriage. No, that isn't freedom to me. That will forever be the "great sadness." But the freedom from the weight that sadness carries.

I will spend the rest of my life knowing that I loved a man—that man—with all of my heart. That a piece of my history will always be his. Not in a way that will inhibit my forward motion. But in a way that has made, well, me. Made me into the woman that I am today. A healthy, vibrant, alive woman. It is also a freedom in knowing that it is okay to live. That though life brought me circumstances I warred against, the Creator of my being has brought me liberty from the war and declared to me that living is okay. So, I'm going to live. And if I never write again regarding my divorce, that is okay. Because spring has arrived, and it has asked me to join it in giving birth to new things and in enjoying the beauty of a season that my heart has missed for so long. And I'm going to enjoy every minute of it!

I met with Ken today. He was telling me this story about his landscaper because I had shared with him what I felt like You had spoken to me regarding the seasons. He told me that his landscaper had said that the first year new plants "sleep." They just get accustomed to their new surroundings and from being out of the place they had been. Then the second year they begin to creep. They begin to feel their way around and dig their roots in firmly. Then the third year they leap. And come to life. "Be mindful of that while you're in this journey," he added.

I shared with him how I had felt that my feelings had shifted regarding my former husband. That this felt like a new season of life; and I told him how excited and grateful I was for all that You have done for me.

"Denise, few people come into my office the way you do, having a heart for the Lord. A real desire to hear Him and walk with Him and not miss Him."

"Really?"

He laughed. "Yeah."

I guess I've looked at people and thought that everyone has a heart for You like I do. So, for whatever reason You've given it to me, Father, I'm grateful. And I ask You to protect it with all diligence from anything that would try to capture it that isn't of You.

"What are you afraid of?" Ken asked.

"You mean, in general, or today?" I like multiple choice.

He laughed.

"I guess I'm most scared of our story just falling out there. I don't want either of us to hurt."

"But what do you know about that?"

"I know that I can't protect either of us anymore, and it might be the very thing that leads to wholeness."

"You're exactly right. But I've told you before, you have to remember that this is your story too. He has a part, but you have a part as well. And if God brings you to a place for you to share it, it's okay for you too."

"I guess I don't want to disrupt the peace with which we've dealt with each other."

"What of that can you control?"

"Absolutely none."

"I'm going to ask you to just invite the Lord in on that part of your heart. On the part that belongs to your story."

And so, Lord, I'm asking You. I'm asking You to lead me on this part of my heart. And if there comes a time for You to have me share my story, You will lead me in quiet confidence in that place.

And obedience to You and You alone. Becoming divorced . . . just
another piece of the journey.

※ ※ ※

I got a heartbreaking email tonight from a friend, telling me the
real state of her marriage. It's broken in what feels like a "humpty
dumpty" kind of way. Where there aren't enough king's horses or
men to put it together again. I feel so responsible, Father. If I had
the tools back then, when they were going through other things,
years ago, I could have given them more. But we didn't have them
for ourselves. I know they still have choices here. And they have to
take responsibility for their own actions, just like I have had to.
But oh, Father, I wish I had known more.

I sent her a long email this morning and then called and talked
to her husband. He sounded okay. He didn't even sound angry. I
gave him the words I felt You had given me—for him to keep his
heart open to You and guard it against the enemy. And that sometimes, moments like these are what actually propel us to wholeness. Grant it, Father, for them, I pray . . . grant them wholeness.

Day 230

I've been reading a book called *The Shack,* and something
struck me in it. That You didn't make women to be completed by
men, which is what so many women think, but You made women
from men, simply out of relationship. The Fall is what made us so
needy. And it caused me to run to You again. To ask You for this
complete completion in You and to know that it will never come
from a person. But it will come beautifully from You and from fel-
lowshipping with You. And whoever You bring me will simply get
to enjoy what You have deposited in the soul of me, and we can
enjoy the gift of a shared journey.

Father, please let me keep this perspective in the years to come.
I know that this season is necessary. I know that what You've asked

of me in regard to trusting You with my finances is because I believe You have given me a calling that will make it necessary for me to be able to trust You for even greater things in the future. There may be a time where I have to step out in faith financially, or something that I don't even know about today, that all of this has been seed planting for. And as long as I know it is You leading, I will be obedient to Your voice.

Questions

Have you been in dating relationships during this season? What has been the outcome of them? What do you believe God has shown you through them? If you haven't had any, what do you feel God's message is to you in that? Are you truly willing to trust God with the relationship He has for you?

Do you have a friend who is going through personal storms right now? What are they? How can you minister to that person in his or her storms?

What are you afraid of right now . . . right at this moment? What of those fears can you control?

What do you believe are things in this season of your life that God is actually teaching you for your future?

Homework

One of the best things to get you out of patterns of self-pity is to begin to think of others who are in need. Spend some time sending notes of encouragements to people you know are also hurting right now. Spend focused time in prayer for them and their needs. And watch how you begin to feel lighter in the process.

I don't know what season this may be for you right now, because
I don't know when you picked up this book. It could be fall, winter, spring or summer. But whatever season it is, you are in it, and
you are alive. So take some time and get out in it. Observe all the
things that are "alive" no matter the season. Chronicle them,
whether in your journal or through the lens of a camera; but take
note. And then go out and enjoy some piece of this season in
some way.

Prayer

*Almighty and most merciful God, we remember before you
all poor and neglected persons whom it would be easy for us
to forget: the homeless and the destitute, the old and the sick,
and all who have none to care for them. Help us to heal those
who are broken in body or spirit, and to turn their sorrow
into joy. Grant this, Father, for the love of your Son, who for
our sake became poor, Jesus Christ our Lord. Amen.*

THE BOOK OF COMMON PRAYER

MONTH 9

EVEN THE DREAMS WE FORGET . . . HE REMEMBERS

(APRIL)

Day 242

Heather called today and said that Matthew was dating someone. I kind of got tickled. She added that she didn't believe he was as spiritually solid as she had thought and that she knew I needed something more for my life. And all I could do was thank You. Thank You for protecting me.

Yesterday I got a call about the house from my former husband. I didn't panic. I am simply trusting You and reminding myself of how You have required me to trust You in every area of my life.

Day 243

I went and auditioned for a commercial today. I know, crazy, right? But I was having dinner the other night with my friend Karol who has a talent agency, and she said, "You know, every now and then I get requests for women your age." I instinctively gave her my raised right eyebrow.

She laughed. "You know, women that could be moms."

"Could be" was the key phrase in that sentence, but I didn't linger there.

"So, if I ever get something that would be good to send you on, would you go?"

I laughed and said in as sarcastic a manner as I could, "Yes, if you ever get one you want to send *me* on, by all means."

And she did. She actually did! It's some commercial for the armed forces network. I have no lines, and she told me to dress the part of a wife who is going to paint a room with her husband. So that is how I dressed. I slapped on a pair of my worn jeans, my tennis shoes and a white T-shirt and orange sweatshirt. I brought a clip in case they wanted me to pull my hair up, and in I walked. I called Mom on my way because I was so nervous and still thought the whole thing was hysterical. But I went anyway.

I get there and there are all these women there who are all dressed up, and here I am dressed like I'm going to paint. I thought, *I'm going to kill Karol.* I had brought *The Shack* with me, because I try to keep a book with me all the time in case I have downtime to actually read. So I was reading, and they finally called my name. I went into this tiny cubby of a room that looked more like a stock room than anything else. There was a bright light, some strange man sitting in a chair who apparently was about to be my make-believe husband, and one "not so happy to be there" lady behind the camera. I assumed she was the director. She shows us our spots and tells us that she will tell us when to go. So she says, "Action," and he and I begin to act out this scene where we get in a paint fight while we're painting a room. When I'm done, Miss "not so happy" is looking pretty happy.

She asks, "Can you pull your hair back? It is kind of in your face and I want to shoot it again so we can see your face."

Well, of course I could . . . I got out my clip as if I traveled with them all the time and flipped my hair up on top of my head and away we went. By the time I left, she was smiling. And I was thinking, *Well, at least she didn't kick me out for the imposter I am.*

I called my mom on the way home and said, "I think the lady actually liked me." Mom just laughed. What a hoot! I haven't done any kind of acting in years, since I did my last few plays in high school. Lord, You never cease to make me smile. And this one today, well, let's just say, You've got a really great sense of humor.

Day 249

I got the commercial! I know, hysterical, right? Karol called and they want me for the commercial. Clincher. It is the same day that

I leave for Maryland to go to Aunt Mill and Uncle Rich's sixtieth wedding anniversary. I tried to see if I could change my flight to fly in later and still make the shoot, but I couldn't do it, and I can't miss this. I had even put those dates down on the sheet I filled out, telling them I couldn't do those dates. But you know what, just knowing I got it is sweet enough for me. I had a feeling that old bird liked me. Lord, You really made me smile today, that is all I have to say.

Day 250

I saw his new place today. He kept my girls for me, and I went to pick them up, and I walked through his place. It is so him. And, thankfully, it wasn't sad for me. Maybe because so little in there had been ours, and everything was his style and what he likes. I think it might have bothered him more seeing me there than it bothered me. There was no sadness when I left, and I had a wonderful drive home.

I'm beginning to feel beautiful too. At the airport I saw a girl who had come to Bible study. We were talking and catching up. She had gone through a divorce this year in what sounded like a similar story and it was a real surprise to me. She said she was headed to meet a male friend. I told her, "Well, whoever gets us at this season in our life will be getting something so much better than a 25-year-old." They will get our wisdom and a much more confident woman.

And that's how I'm beginning to feel in my own skin. Becoming divorced . . . just another piece of the journey.

Day 251

They moved the shoot! The commercial shoot. They completely changed the entire schedule so I could do it. Karol said she has never had that happen. I laughed hysterically into the other end of the phone because, well, it is simply hysterical. Do these people have any idea how long it has been since I have acted? My friends might say not that long, but on a stage, really . . . acting. It's been years. I was sitting there pumping my gas at Sam's when she called me, and I honestly just died laughing.

When I got off the phone I began to thank You for this sweet thumbprint on me. And I just sensed You say, *I haven't even forgotten your little girl dreams.* And then I thought of all the years I wanted to be an actress. Of all the years I spent in the theater company in Charleston, playing Dorothy in *The Wizard of Oz*, doing two years in Piccolo Spoleto, touring in England for three weeks with the theater group and how I always had a secret desire to be as magical as Julia Roberts, even in these later years.

Granted, this won't be Julia Roberts material, but it is still Your sweet thumbprint on my heart. Your sweet, detailed love. I learn more every day that You don't miss anything. You know, if You have made me realize anything through this journey it is that You do care about the details. I have heard ministers debate for years whether or not You truly care about parking places. And I'm not going to lower You to the "Distributor of Parking Places," but I am going to exalt You as a loving Father who cares about every detail of my life.

I have seen it. It can't be denied. If You knew me before I was in my mother's womb; if You carved out my days before one of them was lived; if You know the end before the beginning begins, then You know every piece of my today and tomorrow. And You have fashioned them according to what will bring You the most glory. You remember, too, Father, even the things I forget that mattered to me. If I could help people believe this one beautiful and unimaginable gift, it is this . . . that You know. That You care. That You are present. And that You are in the details. Right smack dab in the details . . .

Day 256

I saw Ken last week. He and I talked through the events of the last month. I told him about my Good Friday conversation with my former husband, and telling him that I was choosing to heal regardless. I told Ken about how I felt when I heard him on the other end of the phone and could tell by the noise and conversations in the background that his life was going on without me, and how that made me feel. I told him about seeing his house and releasing him to find a real love that You created for him.

I also told him that I had started reading John Eldredge's *Wild at Heart*. I told him that I had never claimed my issues in my marriage as a reflection of my value. But I wondered if in another relationship, if something happened that was hurtful, if I would take that on as my own.

Ken looked at me and said, "What did thinking about that make you feel like?"

I said, "It made me feel like I wouldn't be enough."

"You'll never be enough," he said.

And I hadn't really thought about it like that. *I won't ever be enough.*

"And no one will ever really be enough for you," he added.

I settled into that thought. "I hear you. I do. I hear that statement. I think in our humanness we're probably always prone to wonder if we remarry, and then later someone else attracts our eye, think, 'I wonder if I could have gotten him.' "

"Sure, you wonder those things, proving that no one is ever enough. The 'enough' part is only satisfied in one place. With Him."

I think *Wild at Heart* has almost scared me because it so clearly reveals how fundamentally flawed each of us is.

Ken broke into my thought. "I don't want you to discount in any way what you had with your ex-husband. Because I'm sure that what was good was really good. But I honestly believe that you have no idea what is out there for you. And I want it to rock your world. I want you to find someone that rocks your world."

I couldn't help but smile. Because I've thought about that lately. I did express to him my fear of really knowing how to engage that kind of man. But I know part of it is about knowing I'm not in control.

The book also showed me all the ways that I had emasculated him. And I know I did. But I did the best I knew with the tools that

I had to work with. Father, give me wisdom as I enter this new season. Give me the direction and guidance for the new season that You have in front of me. And be with him.

Saturday night Damon and Sarah were over here, and we were talking with my parents. Dad began to unfold to us stories of his childhood and his father. Stories of the brokenness of his own family. We all sat there and listened, asking questions and hearing pieces of our father's history that we had never known. He told us how he had gone to live with my Aunt Mervine when he was pretty young and took care of her three boys when he got home from school. He said they hardly had anything to eat; most days for breakfast and dinner they had grits and eggs and toast and occasionally bacon. Can't help but wonder after all of that why he still loves Cracker Barrel so much, but that is a completely different journal entry. He said the first time he went with my mom to her aunt's house for dinner, he had never seen so much food. He said he ate so much that he embarrassed my mom.

I glanced over at my mom a couple of times, watching as he shared the stories of his childhood, and could see the immense compassion on her face—a compassion that carries her through so much of her own personal story. And in the picture my dad painted, I saw Your rich love. I saw a love that took him from a broken environment, gave him gifts and talents and a woman who loved him, gave him three rather fabulous children. All a reflection of how sweetly You love . . .

Yesterday at church my pastor was preaching, and he was talking about how when husbands and wives aren't intimate there is hardly any greater loneliness, because Your Word has called them to be one flesh. He went on to say that even the unique way that You created our bodies was done so that we could complement each other in a place of oneness. As he was talking about this, I thought of all of those sitting in the pews that know this loneliness. This unspoken place. This place that I've always wished books would talk about and pastors would preach on. Because I am certain that each week there are desperate people sitting in the pews wishing someone would touch on this place of most intimate pain.

I sat there with an ache for those who have suffered this way. For those who have reached across the bed to have their touch rejected. For those who have ached in their body for a spouse who refused to engage their desire. For those who have looked into the face of the one they declared they would submit to and then denied the very place of submission their covenant had vowed. For those who might eventually, for that very reason, or others, find themselves no longer in that marriage, and dwell now in a place of gratefulness that they never have to go back to knowing the pain of being in a marriage that was nothing more than a poor reflection of the amazing gift You had so graciously tried to give. Thank You that my pastor was brave enough to talk about it. May it not be the last time someone does . . .

Day 264

Damon lost his job today. Just a little over a month before baby Georgia is to come into the world. He and Sarah came over today and we went out to the pool. I could see the sense of relief on him because it had been a tough season for him there. I thought of my devotion this morning in all of it. T. D. Jakes said, "There are times in our lives when God will take us from one realm of faith to another. There are multiplicities of fiery trials, but thank God that for every trial there is a faith that enables us. Christ is the Author and the Finisher of our faith. He knows what kind of heat to place upon us to produce the faith needed in the situation. Remember, when we present our bodies as living sacrifices, He is the God who answers by fire. The news lies in the fact that when our faith collapses beneath the weight of unbelievable circumstances, He gives us His faith to continue on . . ."[1]

Father, You have so changed me during this season of my life. I know my faith in You is completely different than what it once was. May this season for Damon and Sarah be a faith-producing one. May we never forget how faithful You are and that Your fiery trials are because You are after our faith . . .

Day 266

I flew into Maryland tonight for Aunt Mill and Uncle Rich's sixtieth wedding anniversary this weekend. It is so good to be here. There are few things I enjoy more in this life than sitting around their little kitchen table, eating her amazing food and being with these people that I so desperately love. She told Mom tonight how good it is to hear me laugh and how grateful she is to see me so happy. Few things in life make me happier than moments like this with them . . .

Day 272

I was a movie star today. Yep, have to admit it. I got to my commercial shoot early and they did my makeup. The stylist helped me pick out my clothes. We chose my green cargo pants, my baby-blue T-shirt and my orange sweatshirt. I put on my baby-blue belt and my tan Nike Rift tennis shoes. And away we went.

Our first scene was shot on a playground. Our second scene we moved down the street and shot at a quaint little white Cape Cod house. There was no Academy Award moment, but there was a lot of sitting around. One of the other actors who played another character kept me cracking up all day. When I finally got to my part of the shoot, I was so nervous. The room was packed, the director and camera were in our face, this strange guy was playing my husband and it all felt, well, a little daunting. But I just took it in. Every moment. I memorized it and enjoyed it. And when it was over I rolled the sunroof open and sang at the top of my lungs all the way home. Today You gave me a piece of Your pleasure. You healed just another little piece of my heart by reminding me that You haven't forgotten even the things that I have.

Questions

What are some closed doors God has given you during this season? Are you able to see now what He might have been trying to accomplish through them? Spend some time thanking Him for even the closed doors.

What is a dream you had forgotten? One that you had packed away in the soul of you? What has God remembered about you?

If you are divorced, one of the hardest things can be watching your former spouse move on. But it is a part of their healing process as well. In what areas do you see your former spouse moving on without you? What is the most painful thing about this for you?

You will never be enough, you know. Not for anyone. And no one will ever be enough for you. What other myths do you think you have believed about yourself or about someone else that you have discovered in this season were simply not true? What other myths have you believed about relationships? What is the real truth about these things that you have come to discover?

Homework

If you don't feel like you're able to do a complete purge right now, that's fine. That ultimately is between you and your heavenly Father. But I would encourage you to at least get rid of one thing this month that you might have held on to for memories' sake. And trust as you do that God never asks you to surrender something that He doesn't have much more for you in return.

You have to read. Yep, I said it. More than this book. Ladies, you have to read a book about men. I suggest *Wild at Heart* because I believe it is truly insightful into the hearts of men. Another one is *Reading Your Male*. Both are powerful books. Gentlemen, you have to read a book about women. *Captivating* is a wonderful book or *Fight Like a Girl: The Power of Being a Woman*. Other books I would suggest are *Listening to Love* and *The Allure of Hope* by Jan Meyer, *The Shack* by Paul Young and *The Silence of Adam* by Larry Crabb.

Prayer

Almighty and eternal God, so draw our hearts to thee, so guide our minds, so fill our imaginations, so control our wills, that we may be wholly thine, utterly dedicated unto thee; and then use us, we pray thee, as thou wilt, and always to thy glory and the welfare of thy people; through our Lord and Savior Jesus Christ. Amen.

THE BOOK OF COMMON PRAYER

Note

1. T. D. Jakes, *Hope for Every Moment: 365 Days to Healing, Blessing and Freedom* (Shippensburg, PA: Destiny Image, 2007).

MONTH 10

IT'S SPRING . . . WHEN GOD BREATHES NEW DREAMS

(MAY)

Day 273

I think this may be the longest I've gone without writing since I began recording my thoughts here. Ken and I had a lot to talk about in our last session. We talked about what I had discovered that evening, listening to my dad share some of his family's story. How I had watched the way my mother took him in while he talked. I told him about some conclusions I had come to over this last month regarding my former husband and how reading *Wild at Heart* had caused me to see some ways I had emasculated him.

"Men are so different from women, Ken."

He laughed. "I'd say."

"Will I know what to do? Will I know how to respond when God brings His man into my life."

"I have no doubt."

This past month has been interesting. Even though my grief over him is gone, I still can hardly talk about him to other people without crying. It just hits such a deep chord with me—the depths of what I felt for him. The shock of how we've walked this out with such love and kindness toward one another and how we are still able to communicate with one another is evident on almost every face. All I can say is thank You for the grace You have given me to walk out this journey. This is only because of You . . .

Day 277

What a wonderful weekend. I was in Dadeville, Alabama, to speak for a women's event on Saturday, and then speak for the morning service on Sunday. They put me up in this quaint little cottage on a golf course. It was so peaceful and sweet. I got in late Friday, and I went with the pastor and his wife to dinner. We had met at Joy Springs back in September, and God had just knit our hearts together so sweetly. We went out to a little place on the lake to eat and they brought me back pretty early so I could rest and get prepared for the event the next morning.

When I woke up on Saturday morning, I went outside to sit on the screened-in back porch that overlooked the golf course. It was so quite and peaceful. It was still pretty chilly, so I wrapped myself up in a blanket and slipped into the rocker and sat my iPhone down beside me to spend some time in prayer. I was planning on talking. I'm good at that, You know. But You asked me to simply listen. I asked You if You were sure. There is still something about me that thinks I have to be doing. Can I really just stop and let You be? Be to me? I know I can. I've felt You so much this year in those moments. They weren't necessarily moments when You asked me to be silent, but moments where I simply couldn't speak. And in those moments You simply spoke to me. But today You asked me for my silence. And I gave it.

It was so refreshing. There was nothing to do but sit there and enjoy You. I enjoyed what You have created. Allowed it to wash through me like a cold Coca-Cola and gave You nothing but a heart that was willing to settle in and appreciate You. I let the music fill the space the sounds of nature hadn't taken over. And then You walked right into the middle of it all. But not the way I expected. It wasn't as I sat there. No, You gave me that time to just enjoy what You had to offer me. As if You had set this meal before me to partake of and didn't require me to even step into the kitchen. But it was when I went upstairs to get ready. I was standing in front of the mirror, putting my makeup on, when the ideas began to come like firecrackers. That is the only way I know to describe them. And it was as if the vision You gave me when I was researching a few years back in Savannah came back to life again for me.

The weekend that I had been working on my second Savannah book and had the attack on my mind regarding how easy it would be to have an affair, something else had happened. I was running and praying, and the hotel where I was sat next door to the new Savannah convention center. As I ran and prayed that morning, I just said out loud, "One day I'm going to come here and we're going to do an event for women that is going to heal the hearts of the women of this city." And just as it came to my mind, I remembered that passage in 1 Samuel 11:1 right before David had his affair with Bathsheba. It says, "In the spring, at the time when kings go off to war, David . . . remained in Jerusalem." And I realized that was one of the reasons he walked headlong into an affair, because he took his eyes off of the purpose You had given him. Just like people take their eyes off of their purpose of being spouses or parents or teachers or pastors.

And so, while I was running that day, You reminded me of my purpose. That same purpose that I believe You have continually reminded me of through the years when the love between he and I had grown so cold that to find someone who would notice me, who would see that I existed and was alive and beautiful, could have taken me to a place that David's leaving his post took him. But You would graciously remind me, even in my most vulnerable and needy times, of my purpose. And it was that purpose that would keep me.

The purpose that I have been called to is to take Your truth to hurting people and remind them of how loving and gracious You are. And in that moment, standing there in front of the mirror, putting my makeup on, the idea for "The Whole Woman Revolution" came to birth in my mind. What You had planted in me all those years ago, running around the Savannah convention center, felt like it came to life right in front of that mirror. And I can't help but wonder if it was all because I had spent that time just abiding in Your presence.

As it poured out in my head from my heart, I could see all of the components come together; and as soon as I did, the insecurities and self-doubt came right behind it. But I still headed downstairs and slipped away to my computer and began to write everything down that was all but taking flight in my head. I finally got all of it down and got in the car and headed to the event. While

I was driving, I remembered how probably five years before I ever wrote *Savannah from Savannah* I had spoken at a church one morning and said, "One day I'm going to write a fiction book about a rigged beauty pageant." Well, at that point, I had never even thought about fiction. But it was so real to me that day. And I did. Five years later, I did. So out loud in the car I said, "One day we will do this and we'll do it in Savannah."

I got to the event and it was perfect, and then Saturday night I was so tired when I got back. But I'm grateful that I didn't stay there alone in the house. Instead, a lady from the church had us over for dinner, where I met this precious 83-year-old woman named Helen. As she and I sat outside and talked while overlooking this beautiful lake, it was as if I got a picture of myself at 83. She was so after God's heart. And so crazy for Him, and I thought, *It doesn't ever have to go away. We can go out just like we are right now.*

Before the evening was over, she asked if she could pray for me. I said, "Sure." I felt that I had gotten to know her enough that I'd let her pray with me before I left. As she began to pray, she spoke over me a beautiful prophetic word: "God has had you from a very little girl. And even the things you wrote down this morning and thought about this morning, God had placed in you years ago." And with those words You beautifully confirmed that all the way back to that day in Savannah, when I was fighting for my purity, You were depositing seed in the soul of me. I have a desire to see lives changed, Father. Lives in my own city. Lives as broken as I've been.

Day 279

I just realized that a year to the day of delivering divorce papers, you delivered a new dream to the heart of me, and I wrote it down right here. One hundred and thirty eight pages later. How good You are! I sent a note to my precious friends who cover me in prayer and just shared with them some of the vision You had given me, asking them to pray over it. Deneen and I had lunch together, and she had a lot of questions for me. I finally told her, "All I have is an idea. Sister doesn't have anything other than that." She didn't ask me any more questions.

Ken and I talked about it at my appointment today. I took him all the way back to the experience in Savannah to this weekend, and everything I felt like You had spoken to me. I told him about Miss Helen's prayer. I shared with him how I had been thinking about it and processing it.

"I really sense in my heart, Denise, that this is from God. Since your heart has come alive to the Lord, it is like you have been un-corked and the things of God are able to freely flow through you."

"You know, Ken, the person sitting in front of you today isn't the same person who sat down in front of you a year ago."

"I know that."

We both sat in that for a moment. *A year . . . my, my.*

"Why don't you take this vision and spend a couple of weeks just clipping pictures out of magazines that connect with your heart and what you feel this looks like. Make a big collage almost as a catalyst for a brainstorming retreat. Then get away for a weekend and get you a large pad and write down everything you see regarding this vision."

I started thinking immediately of where I could go. Maybe back to the little cabin or to my friend's house at the beach. Just sitting there, I couldn't wait to do it. It's like I'm expecting or something. What would this look like for my life?

"The question to answer, Denise, is 'Why should this matter?' And 'Why do people miss seeking out their wholeness?' "

I knew that was the real question. It was for my own journey. We went back to the squirrel story he had told me months ago. The squirrel wanted food. He was hungry. But fear kept him away. Just like fear is what keeps us away. Our fear of being completely honest: with ourselves, with God, with others.

"Have I ever told you about the picture God gave me about the ocean?" He asked.

"Nope."

"I had this picture of how 95 percent of the church was standing on the beach looking at the beautiful ocean. And they were talking about how beautiful it was, but they weren't getting in it. It was like they were thinking, *Someone else will do it. I like the view from here.* And I was wondering, *Why are they just standing there?*

"Then there were a few who waded in; but as soon as the waves rushed in they would run back. They were afraid.

"But others dove down and they couldn't come up for air. And God was saying, 'I'll be your air; breathe in deeply.'"

"But to do that means we're no longer in control. It means we'll drown," I said.

"Exactly, it means you'll drown."

And in that moment, I knew that is what You desire, Father. Because You need us to completely die in order for You to live and become completely alive in us. Thank You that You are alive in me; and I promise, Father . . . I'm willing to drown. If that is what it takes, I'm willing to drown.

"You know, Ken, I've been around people for a long time who are big talkers. It is as if they need to paint these elaborate pictures of things that are so far from reality in order to feel approved. And yet, when the things don't come to pass it heightens the pain and the embarrassment. I don't want people to view me as some big talker."

"You need to walk away from that fear," Ken said. "That is not yours, and it doesn't matter how people view you. It matters that God trusts you and that you believe in Him. And He believes in you."

And I do, Father. I so know that You are a safe place to land. Thank You for how You spoke to me today and for validating my ability to hear You. I feel so completely alive right now, and I'm so grateful for this season that there are no distractions in my way to pull me from You. Thank You for this day, for this season. Thank You that I will not watch. I will not wade. I will drown.

Becoming divorced . . . just another piece of the journey.

Day 280

I've been thinking a lot about incubation periods today. I always wanted children. You know that. But it wasn't a piece of this season of my journey. But I thought about how during that season of incubation so much is going on that we can't see underneath that belly.

There have been moments, Father, when I have felt guilty for how good You've been to me through this. How You have kept me in my home, provided for my needs, given both him and me the ability to walk this out, so far, with grace and kindness. How You have healed my heart. But what I realize is that I have been incubating. And what looks like such a sweet season right now is nothing but a harvest of incubation. A baby will eventually be born. A healthy baby will be born if we don't force it out too soon. And that is what all of these years have been for me. (Though I wish the whole "a year is like a day" thing wasn't how You worked, because some of these years have been long!)

But in all of these years, I have been persistently moving back toward You. Even when I was hurt or angry or had suffered another broken desire or unmet expectation, and I had to recalibrate . . . I always recalibrated back to You. I never let the pain of what I was going through rob You from me. You were the perpetual constant, and I was the perpetual "presser inner." I didn't want to miss You. I was like Your disciple Peter, when he said, "Where else would I go?" And while I was doing all of that thrashing back and forth, things were happening. Life was growing. And it feels like I've finally been born, that all of that was for all of this. This real life I am experiencing now.

I'm still uncertain of where we're headed. I'm still uncertain of what this baby will look like. But what I am certain of is that fruit takes time, babies take time, dreams take time, healing takes time . . . and You ain't ever in a hurry . . .

Day 286

Today, a year to the date of starting this journal, I joined my church. I became a part of their mosaic. Damon went forward with me. I started this with him, so it was so nice to have him there.

My pastor's wife came up and hugged me, and we talked for a while. Then my pastor prayed over me and thanked You for the woman that I was. It was a precious prayer. But as I sat there tonight it was a bittersweet moment for me.

Starting over means that I am leaving something behind. New beginnings represent the end of something. But You were so sweet in that moment. Your presence was so real. And as I looked around at the faces in that service that I didn't even know, splattered with a few familiar, I realized that these are the people I am going to be doing life with. That You will use me here. I know that. And so tonight, Father, I thank You for my new family . . .

Day 290

It's so weird how grief can sweep over me in a moment and I don't even know where it comes from. Last night I had the radio on while I was driving home, and Garth Brooks' song "The Dance" came on. Okay . . . now I know where it comes from! And I started crying. Then when I got home, I looked at our pictures that are laying in my armoire facedown and thought, *This isn't how it should have been. I shouldn't have been in this bed alone for the last year.* I cannot believe it has been a year since he left. It's amazing how quickly time flies, and yet my emotions can still feel so fresh.

In the song, Garth Brooks says that he is glad that he didn't know the way everything would end, because while he would have missed the pain, he would have also had to "miss the dance." There are days I would be grateful to have missed this dance. The pain of this dance anyway. But if I had to live it all over again—every heartache, every unfulfilled promise, every time my heart broke— I would do it all again. There were good things tucked in the middle of it. It wasn't all bad. There were things that were sweet and kind, and there was laughter in the middle of it all too. But in spite of what I have gone through, I would do it all again. I would do it all again because it brought me here. It brought me to this place with You. It brought me to this sweet moment of my life. So, no,

Father, I wouldn't miss the dance. I wouldn't have wanted to miss it at all.

Last night I was out with Deneen for Andrew's birthday. I was observing a friend of hers and was just listening to him talk and watching how he interacted with me, and it made me once again fear being relearned. I know that I was never completely known by my former husband. I know that more clearly now than I did when this journey began, in part because I shut myself down so much that what he got from me was not completely my real heart. He got my wounded heart, my insecure heart—the heart that I allowed our circumstances and our stuff to create in me. My prayer, Father, is that the man that I get to spend this next chapter of my life with will bring out the best parts in me. Accentuate them. Complement them. And walk out my wholeness with me. That is my prayer.

Day 291

The last few days have been harder than they have been in a while. I think encountering Deneen's friend the other night freaked me out a little. The way he interacted with me created something in me that made me want to run back to what I knew. Really kind of scary to actually see myself write that down.

I found myself crying yesterday over the fact that we would never have children together yet again, that we'd never raise *our* children. You know what is so crazy is that there were so many ways we complemented each other. Yes, I know the reality of that statement, and that there were many ways that we didn't that were horrifically difficult. Shoot, maybe this is why I need to write it down at all . . . to get perspective. But today I missed him. I just missed talking to him, being with him. And sometimes it feels completely impossible to believe that he won't be a part of my future, that our future together stopped at this time a year ago. Or maybe it's not him at all. Maybe it is simply missing what is familiar. Comfortable. Seemingly known.

Father, I truly don't want any distractions. I was distracted for so long—so consumed with trying to keep my marriage together—that in the middle of that I was falling apart. I won't allow grief or these emotions to settle in on me and distract me from the new vision You've placed inside of me. I know the enemy would love nothing more than to steal the joy in this season that You are birthing new things. I haven't had to fight the enemy in a while. It is as if there has been this beautiful hedge of protection, and now these emotions feel like a distraction. Thank You for this revelation tonight, Father. Thank You for letting me take the time to sit here and write it out. In doing that I've found a truth I needed to see. The devil will always be out to steal my joy.

Continue to help me walk this road as I must. Help me live it as You've called me to; and bring more healing every day . . . this is all I know to pray.

Day 294

He came by today to get some more of his clothes. As he loaded up trash bags and removed more of his life from our home, I sat on the floor beside the closet and watched him fill his bags. We talked about the business and how it was going. Every now and then he asked about me, and I shared my life in sound bites. Maybe that is why being alone isn't as difficult as it could be. There wasn't a lot of sharing my deep places through the years, so even now it doesn't feel like I have a lot to talk about.

When he left, he just held me. And when he went to leave, he gave me that look. The one that said, "I love you." I do know what it looks like. Even though it has been a long time since I've seen it. He texted me after he left and told me how good it was to see me, and that he still loves me. I told him the same and that nothing will change that. And nothing will. I will always love him. I know that.

Day 295

I had a slight breakdown this morning. I forgot to feed my girls last night but didn't realize it until I got up this morning, and it completely freaked me out. Every now and then I'll have these feelings that I'm sinking again. But I honestly believe this is more of a spiritual battle. I have had to do a lot of pouring out lately. And I think it has intensified the assault on me, which I'm thankful to say forces me to press in harder to You. But it also happens so often when you bring new dreams. It is kind of like the parable of the sower and the seed. The enemy will do whatever he can to snatch the seed away. And the cares of this world are one of his best weapons.

It's easy to get distracted with where I am and lose sight of where You desire to take me. It's easy to allow the pain of this past year to wrap itself around me again, like a noose, and miss all that You have done in the middle of the pain. It is the choosing piece . . . You know, choosing to look at this as "how good You are for bringing, in one of the darkest times of my life, the sweetest reflections of Your love." Instead of looking at this as "when I could be experiencing You in such sweet ways, instead I am having to endure all of this pain." So I choose to let You be the focus here. And I choose not to allow the enemy to rob the seed of newness of life that You have planted inside my heart in this season of spring.

So, this morning, after I pulled it back together, I was praying and asked You to protect my heart even from him. He is probably the place where I am most vulnerable. The place I want to run to when I get lonely. When I want to share something or want to have a conversation with someone, he's the one I want to have it with. Even though so much of that piece didn't work well.

Yesterday, I asked Damon and Sarah if someone would ever love me. Damon said, "More than you've ever been loved." Then I asked, "But will I love him?" And he said, "More than you ever thought you were capable of loving." I don't know that I am capable of loving anyone more than I love him. I don't know how that is possible. But all I know is that you have given me a promise in my heart that You will bring someone into my life. And all I can do is trust that when he does come into my life, the depth and breadth of his love will crowd out the aching of what I've lost. And that it will so surpass what I've known that I will be amazed.

This morning I laid my head back on my pillow and tried to imagine actually telling someone my whole story. I thought of how the choices I have made over the last 15 years have caused me to live with this story for the rest of my life. But if I looked at it as consequences for my choices, then that would mean I made a mistake in marrying him. And I still don't believe that is true. There is so much today that I know I don't have answers to. So much of this journey that I've traveled that I don't understand and am unable to fully wrap my mind around Your purpose or plan in it. But what I do know, Father, is that without You, I would have never made it. And I am confident that You have a plan for even the things I cannot see.

Day 300

Tonight might be the night! Sarah started having contractions when we were at the concert on the lawn. Somewhere in the middle of listening to the eighties band that was on the schedule for the night sing their rendition of "Billie Jean" and "Maniac," she began having contractions. Not sure if my laughter was appropriate for her pain, but I can't wait until this little one gets here. I'm looking forward to everything about it.

I'm looking forward to the fact that I'm going to get to do life with this little one. That one day she's going to ask her mommy and daddy if she can go home with Aunt Niecy. That one day she's going to cry because she doesn't want me to leave her house after I've visited. That she's going to know that a trip with Aunt Niecy means a trip to McDonald's, and that all of her best memories I'll get to be a part of. So, in spite of Sarah's pain, I laughed.

Bring the little one in safely, Father . . . bring her in safe.

Day 310

No Georgia. Little stinker.

Questions

What are some of the new visions God has planted in your heart during this season? What are some of the things that you feel you are coming alive to?

As you begin to look back over this "almost a year of your life," what are some of the ways you feel God can use your pain? How have you seen Him use your pain even during this season?

Remember Ken's story about the people who simply stood and stared at the ocean . . . then those who waded in . . . then those who dove in? Are you willing to dive into the depths of God's love? If not, what is keeping you from it? And what do you think you are missing from totally abandoning your heart, your pain, your dreams and your pictures to Him?

What are some things that have been in a season of incubation in your life? Just like new moms and dads prepare for the arrival of the baby during those nine months the baby is safely inside its mother's womb, what do you feel like God has had you doing to prepare for your "delivery"? Is it in your heart? Your spirit? Your thoughts? Have you been tempted to help Him out? To try to deliver it faster? What is the danger in this? How can you give this back to Him and trust Him for the perfect day of delivery?

Homework

Spend some time simply enjoying Jesus this week. Don't feel the pressure to take your needs, concerns and requests to Him. Just spend some time enjoying Him, delighting in Him. And then during the rest of your day listen closely to the things He desires to speak to you.

Is there a vision of some kind in your heart? Then put together a vision board. Buy some of your favorite magazines, a piece of poster board and glue sticks and scissors, and cut out any visual or word that captures you and what is in your heart. Make your own collage and use it as a catalyst for what God has placed in the soul of you. Later, when you can, take a spiritual retreat alone with the Lord and chart out what all of it looks like. You will be amazed at what God will reveal.

Prayer

Almighty and eternal God, so draw our hearts to thee, so guide our minds, so fill our imaginations, so control our wills, that we may be wholly thine, utterly dedicated unto thee; and then use us, we pray thee, as thou wilt, and always to thy glory and the welfare of thy people; through our Lord and Savior Jesus Christ. Amen.

THE BOOK OF COMMON PRAYER

MONTH 11

WHEN LIFE
BREAKS THROUGH

(JUNE)

Day 304

Still no Georgia . . . but her nursery is ready. And it is beautiful. Brown and pink and all ready for her arrival. The furniture is in place. I finally found the perfect pink piggy bank I had been searching for months for. So everything is in its place but her. Another sweet piece of life and a beautiful gift to balance the death this past year brought.

As I sat on her floor for a few minutes today, I grieved for myself. There have been moments when watching Sarah's excitement or feeling Georgia kick from inside her mommy's womb that the pain has swept through me. The baby book is still upstairs in my drawer, and the Beatrix Potter mobile and little height measurer that I bought the first year of my marriage are up in the closet. The little knit outfit in cream that my mother bought and gave me years ago is upstairs stashed in another drawer. And the pink Chinese pajamas I bought on our first cruise 13 years ago rests in yet another. Each one a stinging reminder of what could have been . . . what should have been . . . what will never be with him.

And in the middle of this sweet and exciting time is the bittersweet reminder that Georgia will never be mine. She won't come out with my eyes or my nose. She will be her mama's and daddy's. And I wonder . . . I wonder what You have for me, Father. In the world of parenting . . . in the joy of being a mother . . . in the journey of this life, what does my journey hold for me?

There have been many tears cried over this ache in my soul. There have been many moments when the desire to be called mom, to see a reflection of me outside of myself, has been sweeping and overwhelming. But there is a settledness in me as well. That You have a good plan. A good plan. Thank You for letting me enjoy this new journey of my brother and sister-in-law's life. Thank You that I am here to see it, experience it and rejoice with them in it.

I read a devotional once in *Streams in the Desert* where it talked about the real gift of patience is when we celebrate another's joy while our own desires go unfulfilled. It is easy to celebrate in their joy, Father. And it is even easier to trust that You have every piece of mine firmly in the palm of Your hand. I don't know where, when, how or what . . . but I know that every piece of my joy, every piece of Your plan, will unfold perfectly for me . . .

Becoming divorced . . . just another piece of the journey.

Day 305

Damon and Sarah came to sit with me by the pool today. Not sure if it was a last-ditch effort at their freedom before the consuming world of infanthood attaches itself to them, or if it was to entertain themselves so they can get through this agonizing wait. She's killing us!

Sarah said she has had more contractions. And while we were at the pool, she had even more. We had a sweet day though. We sat with our feet dangling in the water; we laughed and talked and ate and waited on the arrival of new life. And in the middle of it all, You are so very present.

Day 306

I'm sitting here looking at Sarah in the hospital bed. I got the call about 6:00 this morning to meet them at the hospital and pick up Toto—Sarah's little Yorkshire terrier and Damon's sacrifice for love. So I picked up Toto, carried him to my house to hang with his cousins, and grabbed my already packed bag (yes, *I* had a packed bag) and headed back to the hospital. Both sets of grandparents are on their way, because they, too, have been sitting on go. And now I'm watching Sarah munch on ice chips and act like we ain't about to have a baby!

Damon is walking around with the video camera and acting all but giddy. The nurse isn't the sweetest thing ever, so we're looking forward to the shift change. But it looks like sometime today Georgia is coming!

❋   ❋   ❋

She has arrived! Georgia Ryan is here. The text just came through. She is almost two feet long and came in weighing a burly 8 pounds and 10 ounces. Both sets of grandparents got here just in the nick of time and brought my oldest niece, Hannah, along too. Sarah's dad said that as big as Georgia is she's liable to walk through the door and introduce herself. We have laughed at Sarah and Damon's franticness as first-time parents. And we have squealed with delight like giddy school girls over the arrival of this sweet miracle. We'll get to go see her in a minute after the new family has had time to take in their moment. A moment that every new family deserves . . .

❋   ❋   ❋

She is perfect. Perfectly beautiful. And looks just like Damon. I mean, the spitting image. It is unbelievable. I think it is Your gift to me too. Since he and I hated each other most of my life, it is like I'm getting a do-over, and this time I'll get to like him. The day was sweet. Capped off with a Steak 'n' Shake burger and fries. We couldn't have asked for anything else. This is the beginning of a new journey with this little one. Thank You that she came out safe and healthy, Father. Thank You that You are the giver of life. And thank You that You let us share in the miracle of it . . . it was a pleasure.

Day 322

It's been quite a while since I've written. Huge progress. I even went right past my anniversary, the first one not being married, and it turned out to be such a wonderful day—so wonderful that there was no pain to journal in it. There was such a sweetness of Your presence in that entire day. I've started doing something a little different too. I haven't done it since I was a child. I've started kneeling by my bed at night when I say my prayers. Just thanking You for my day. Praying over my dreams. Covering my family. You have given me some of the sweetest times I've had in so long. And the addition of Georgia has just made all of it sweeter. And I just want to thank You in a different way.

So, thank You for how You've met me by my bed. You have been so kind to me, so loving, and Your presence has been so sweet. And I continually feel You speaking more and more to my heart regarding vision. At each new step, You speak a "how." And I am grateful.

I'm meeting with him today. It is about money. I'm not fearful. I'm just going to be honest and trust You will lead our discussion and know that at the end of the day You are my supply. You will provide for every need that I have, regardless of what the conduit is to get it to me.

Thank You for all that You are doing in me. Thank You for all You have been to me. Thank You for the provision of every need that I have during this season. Thank You for my family and new baby Georgia. Thank You for work this summer as I start to teach Creative Writing to kids. And thank You that You are working in every aspect of my life. I'm so grateful that You are ever present on this journey.

Questions

In divorce so many things are lost. What are the greatest losses that have resulted from your divorce?

In the middle of seasons that feel like death, God still brings gifts of life. What are some of the gifts of life that He has brought to you during this season? If you can't recognize them, ask Him to allow you to see what is causing you to miss seeing His gifts of life. And then listen, because He will reveal it if you really desire to see it.

How has going through this year of "firsts" affected you? What were the hardest firsts? Why? What were the easiest? Why?

What are some of the new relationships that God has brought into your life during this season? What have they afforded you? What have you afforded them?

Homework

Send a note to the "new" relationships God has given you this year, telling them the gift they have been to you and how you see God's love in providing them to you during this season of your life.

Try kneeling by your bed at night to say your prayers. Or, if you don't want to kneel, lie down, but give Him the last part of your day. And when you wake up, give Him the first part. Before the television is turned on, before the first cup of coffee or first Coke is drunk, give it to Him. You have started a new journey. Begin and end it with Him . . .

Prayer

O Lord, support us all the day long, until the shadows lengthen, and the evening comes, and the busy world is hushed, and the fever of life is over, and our work is done. Then in thy mercy, grant us a safe lodging, and a holy rest, and peace at the last. Amen.

THE BOOK OF COMMON PRAYER

MONTH 12

GONE FISHIN'

(JULY)

Day 335

I was reading my devotional this morning. The Scripture reference was Revelation 3:7, where John writes to the church at Philadelphia. It's the passage that says God opens doors that no man can shut and shuts doors no man can open, revealing so clearly that our closed doors are just as much You as our opened doors. I've believed this from the beginning of this journey—with Matthew, with my books, with this house not selling. The doors that have closed this year are because You have closed them. I'm so grateful for Your great love and for Your great protection over my life.

Farther down in that devotional the writer said, "If God allows a relationship to continue, and some negative painful betrayals come from it, you must realize that He will only allow what ultimately works for your good. Sometimes such a betrayal ushers you into the next level of consecration, a level you could never reach on your own. For that we give thanks!"[1]

I've thought this more than once throughout this journey. I've always felt like I truly prayed over whether he was the man I was to marry. I felt as if You confirmed that he was. And that makes me wonder if the journey of the last 15 years, and now this past year of walking through this divorce, if it hasn't been for a higher purpose. You knew where You were taking me. My new level of consecration to You is simply undeniable. And like Joseph's imprisonment, You planned it. You orchestrated it. I'm not saying this to be a martyr. But I am asking the question, knowing that You allow things for a reason. Could it be that there was a reason bigger than me, for the larger glory of Your kingdom?

Day 350

Another birthday, ugh . . . wish I could put a stop to them. But seeing that the only alternative is death, I'll settle for being another year older. I'm making a funny! Wonder if I've made many funnies over this year? I was reading my entry from my birthday last year. My, I can't even feel those emotions now. They are foreign to me. If they hadn't been written down I couldn't re-create them now. And how grateful I am that they aren't a part of my daily journey anymore.

I had my appointment with Ken yesterday. He asked me if I was wild. I initially said no. Then I paused and really thought about it and said, "You know, I think I am. I've always wanted to be on the *Amazing Race*. I just think that would be a blast, even though you'd have to knock me out to do 90 percent of what they do, because I'm so afraid."

And then I said, "I'm afraid of so much. I've spent so much time being afraid: afraid of what people will think, afraid my husband would leave. Afraid of so much. I'm tired of being afraid. I think that is why I loved Donald Miller's book *Blue Like Jazz*, because he isn't afraid of what I'm going to think when I'm holding that book in my hands. And some moments he makes me laugh until I cry. Other moments I want to throw the book across the room. But the beauty is that he is living so transparently. So real. Regardless of what people think . . . and I want that."

He just looked at me and smiled the way he does.

"I think I want to start talking about where I've walked. I haven't wanted to share any of this for so long, Ken, because I haven't wanted it to define me. I haven't wanted it to be the whole of my story. But I've realized it isn't. This is only a piece of my story, a piece that is making me who I am."

He scooted up in his chair and leaned in to me. "You know, Denise, I can count on one hand, possibly two, in 17 years of practice, the people who have walked this journey out well; and you are one of those people. You haven't been afraid to go to any place you've needed to in your heart or your pain to be whole."

I leaned back in my chair and gave him my smile. The smile that says, "Me? You're talking about me?"

He laughed.

I said, "I saw that in Paul Young, the man who wrote *The Shack*. He was willing to press into his healing. A healing his counselor told him would take 18 months and that few ever finished, and he did it in 9 months. And look what came out of it."

"Yep, look what came out of it."

"There was a girl who wrote me a letter recently, talking about my books and how she loved them, and she was asking about my marriage and about him, and how she loved the songs we had written. I told her about my divorce, and then a couple days later I get this Google alert, and she's blogged about my divorce. I can't tell you how violated I felt with that."

"I can imagine."

"This is something *I* want to share, Ken. I think there is a book in this about walking out this journey. About being completely connected to my heart and to God in the middle of this intense pain. But I can't write it until I'm willing to talk about it. To tell it."

"No, you can't."

"You know, I still feel like my life is in complete chaos. I don't have a marriage; I don't have a book deal. I have pretty much no income. I share the ownership of a house with a man, tying me to him, that has been on the market for over a year. And yet, in the middle of all of this, my heart is so at rest. It's like the Lord has let me know this is God-controlled chaos. I feel like I've finally come to that 'Storm Proof' place that I have taught other people about for the last three years. Storms are everywhere. Uncertainty is everywhere. But I am so certain that He has a perfect plan, so certain that I have a great future, so certain that I am exactly where He has me. Because He has been involved with every detail of my life. Every detail."

I feel that You are continuing to say to me, *Be still and know*. And this is what I know:

I know that You are God.

I know that You care about every detail of my life.

I know that You have a good plan for me.

I know that I have been assigned an anointing to destroy the works of the devil.

I know that something is on the horizon of my life.

I know that You are a light to my feet and a lamp to my path.

I know that there is a calling on my life, and You will advance me in Your kingdom in Your time and in Your way.

I know that I will continue to diligently live out this life You've given me. Trusting You all the way.

And I know that I plan on staying 39 forever! I can't be older than my mother anyway!

I also had another revelation this morning while reading John Eldridge's book. He was talking about "agreements" again. Agreements we make with the enemy. And I realized I had made an agreement that "No one could love me completely." Not everything about me. Even to the point where I thought, *I won't let whoever I marry see me without eye makeup. They won't like me then.*

But I heard You say, *Oh, baby girl, can't you see that this is what this entire year has been about? Showing you how completely I love you and that there isn't one piece of your heart or your fears or your longings or your joys that I don't want to share in? You are loved. So completely loved.*

Thank You, Lord, that I break that agreement. That one day I will be loved so well, but I am already loved completely. You are so precious to me, Father. And thank You that You are the first place I go . . .

Day 358

So last night I was getting ready to go meet Ashley and Lawana for my first trip to a bar! I'm 39, and this is my first trip to a real bar. Okay, not because I've always had some secret desire to go to a bar, but because Ashley's boyfriend plays there and she wanted Lawana and me to hear him. So I'm getting ready, and my real estate agent calls me wanting to know if he can do an open house on Sunday. Well, I almost freaked out on the phone. Just the mere mention of it sent me to this overwhelmed place that I haven't known in a very long time. I should have identified it right away because it's the same feeling I always get right before I start a new Bible Study. Except that before, I had him to talk through it with me, and he wasn't there. In fact, there has been a huge shifting this year of allowing You to go to those places with me and bringing You into them before I bring anyone else into them. You meet me right where I am in the middle of them, but I have to invite You into that pain. I have to call on You before I call on anyone else, and You've so taught me how to do that this year. You've taught me how to really ask You and talk to You about anything.

I completely fell apart after I got off the phone, and I leaned over the kitchen island, asking You, "Where is this coming from? What is this emotion all about?" And the whole way in the car I was praying and talking to You and surrendering anything and everything. Surrendering my calling, the books You've given me to write, the Bible study—just laying it all down—and yet I don't feel like You're asking me not to do any of it. So I keep asking. On the ride back home I'm asking. In the middle of the night, when I wake up, it's on my mind, and I'm asking You again.

In the morning, when I get up, I ask You again. Then, as I'm reading John Eldridge's book, I come to these words: "Don't just assume the attack you are under on any given day is yours. It might be someone else's battle, trying to transfer to you, sometimes it comes beforehand, trying to take you out so that you don't even offer any help."

That was when I realized this was an attack to overwhelm me so I would quit something. So I would stop working on something and just say, "That's too much. I can't do that." But instead, I realized that "I can do all things through Christ who strengthens me" (Phil. 4:13, *NKJV*). That "the steps of a good man are ordered by the LORD, and He delights in his way" (Ps. 37:23, *NKJV*). You spoke that clearly to me this morning in my prayer. Your word to me wasn't, *Be still and know.* This morning Your word was, *The steps of a good man are ordered by the LORD, and He delights in his way.*

I was so grateful for realizing what this was about. But it still hovered over me all day like a shadow. It was awful. I didn't even

want to cook dinner. I didn't want to leave the house. I just wanted
to fall into bed. So, I got up and began to pray against it. Even
though it was still so heavy on me. I didn't even feel like I could fight
my way out of it. But boy, did You minister to me there. And even
though I didn't feel it leave, and I still didn't want to leave the house,
I made myself. And that one act lifted me out from under that heaviness. Not giving into it, but walking out of it. Sometimes we have to
walk out of things. Like Deneen says, "Emotion follows action."
Man, how true have I found that to be through the years!

So, thank You so much, Lord, for being the first place I turn to.
Before I pick up the phone, I go to the throne, like my friend Paige
says. Thank You, Lord, for letting that be true in my life. I pray that
I will continue to do that even after You bring me a partner to share
these remaining years with. That this will be a new way of life for me.
That You will stay at the center of my heart and my joy. And that
You, before any man, or any person, will be the first place my heart
goes to seek refuge.

Now, back to our evening . . .

When Lawana and I got to Ashley's, she looked at me and said,
"I've got some clothes to give you."

"What?"

"Yes, I've got some clothes I don't wear anymore, so I want to
give them to you."

For the next 30 minutes, I watched as she loaded up a huge bag
with eight pairs of jeans, six T-shirts and two jackets. I was amazed.
First, because no one has ever given me clothes. For the last few years
at the end of each season I have pulled clothes from my closet that I
haven't worn in at least two years and found someone to give them
to. And besides my mom and Joan, no one has ever just given me
clothes. And then I thought of the fast. And I thought of all the
clothes Mom and Joan have bought me this year. And now this. This
bag full of clothes. And I hear You saying once again, "All I want to
do is provide for you . . ." And provide for me you have.

Now, to our interesting evening at the bar.

I love to people watch. I am mesmerized by the things people
do. And I had no idea this place would be quite so full of characters.

We got a table up at the edge of the balcony where we could see the stage well and watch all the people. My word, I saw everything. I saw one girl flitter through three men before I had finished half of my Coke. I saw a group of guys with baseball caps on who looked like guys I went to college with, yet 20 years later. I saw people dancing, seducing, desperate. Some were just having innocent fun. Some were drunk off their rockers. Some were talking to strangers, connecting worlds that only moments before had been foreign.

Sitting there, I remembered a story Pastor Rice told about when he used to be a bouncer at a bar. He said that about three o'clock in the morning, when all of the lights would come up, and people could actually see what that person really looked like that they had just spent their entire evening with, they were like, "Oh . . . oh my. Well, gotta run." I laughed, thinking that well after I left, there would probably be a lot of "Oh mys" going on.

It's also interesting that I am moving past my fear. My old self wouldn't have come through this door out of fear of what people would think. The author and Bible study teacher in a bar? What? But I am living out my authentic design. My buddy's boyfriend plays in a country band that tonight is playing at a bar on Broadway, and I'm going to listen to him. I'm going to drink a Coke and sit up there and people watch and enjoy this moment with my friends. My, how far I have come!

Lawana and I began to wonder if this would have been the kind of place You would have come to when You were on the earth. I honestly can't imagine that if You had heard all the commotion going on as You passed by that You wouldn't have stopped. I could see You walking in, smiling and then homing in on the heart that needed You the most. You would ask a few questions. Offer some precious words of life.

Do I have that same ability? That same discernment? I know You live in me, and I know I could see the desperation of so many tonight, but I didn't minister to any of them. I simply observed.

Another interesting event tonight was meeting a friend of Ashley's. He had a sweet heart. He walked us to our car and got in the way of two drunken guys who had come up on us pretty fast and furious. And when we dropped him off at his car, there were a few drops of rain that had begun to fall on my windshield, and he said, "Now, y'all be careful driving in this weather."

His sense of protection struck me. So on the drive home, You and I were talking, and I asked You to give me someone that cared where I was. That cared that a couple drops of rain had fallen on my windshield. It's interesting to learn more and more what I truly desire. Thank You for allowing me to get glimpses of what You desire me to have.

Day 366

Well, it's been a year. I'm closing it out. Hanging up the "gone fishin'" sign for all to see. There will be no more counting firsts—marking monuments of holidays no longer celebrated. No more one-year anniversaries to this grief. I've officially "gone fishin'." That was my declaration this morning in my prayer to You. This is over. No more remembering or counting days. The year marker has come, and tomorrow begins a new season. I'm believing that this Thanksgiving, this Christmas are going to be marked with a newness.

Just as I leave tomorrow for my spiritual retreat back to the little cabin in Alabama, where You gave me this new vision, I believe this is the beginning of a truly "new" season for my life. I thank You for all I've learned this year. I thank You for what You've revealed to my heart and to my eyes. I thank You for how You've provided for me and walked with me and loved me in my details. And I thank You that our relationship is forever changed. I will never walk with You the same again. This has been the sweetest time of my life. For that I am grateful. But this new year, we're going even further. Digging even deeper. Learning even more. Seeing even greater revelations. Taking even larger steps of faith.

Thank You for the peacefulness of this day. I honestly haven't even thought about it much. Had it not been for Bobbie and Mom calling this evening, I don't know that I would have thought about this being the year anniversary of my divorce.

This past season will always be a part of my life but not a part of my future. I am now pushing the dirt over any monument to my past. And no monument to the past will ever be resurrected. It is as if the grass has finally grown over the grave and there is hardly any recognition of when the burial occurred. But there will be no making idols here.

Thank You for Your healing. Thank You for Your companionship. Thank You for Your grace for that moment and season that I prayed would never come, but came anyway. You were in it. When I got there, You were there. You are Jehovah-shammah—"The Lord God is there." And You have proven it to me.

I'm so grateful that You were a constant companion for me today. And even on the days when I haven't even known how to talk to You, I know You've known my heart and have been very present through all of it. And for that I am so grateful. I love You with all my heart. Thank You for helping me get through today. I pray You will continue to heal both him and me and bring us into Your perfect will for each of us. Wherever that may be.

But I'm expecting amazing things.

Here is my excerpt from last year. I declared it then and I know it now . . .

When the Lord brought back the captive ones of Zion, we were like those who dream. Then our mouth was filled with laughter and our tongue with joyful shouting. . . . The LORD has done great things for us; we are glad. Restore our captivity, O LORD, as the streams in the South. Those who sow in tears shall reap with joyful shouting. He who goes to and fro weeping, carrying his bag of seed, shall indeed come again with a shout of joy, bringing his sheaves with him (Ps. 126, *NASB*).

Amen and amen.

I am divorced . . . and it is only a piece of my journey.

Note

1. T. D. Jakes, *Hope for Every Moment: 365 Days to Healing, Blessing and Freedom* (Shippensburg, PA: Destiny Image, 2007).

EPILOGUE

As a writer you never really finish a story, you just choose to stop. You have to at some point. This story is pretty much the same. It didn't end on day 366. In fact, it still hasn't. There is residue that this experience still flings to the surface and requires me to face, deal with and heal from. But it has still been a beautiful journey.

As I began to go back over my journals to write this book, my heart was at such a different place. Yet, there were moments that reading the words on these pages were as fresh as when I had written them. And there were other moments when the feelings were foreign, as if they had been in another life or lived by another person. That is the essence of healing, I guess.

And healing I have done. My relationship with my former husband hit some bumps in the road. There was a brief season when the kindness we had shared wasn't quite so kind anymore, giving me a glimpse into another realm of divorce—the cruel side—yet offering me another layer of compassion to those crushed by the weight of this evil epidemic. But we have now severed every tie and let each other go with the same dignity we came into this relationship with. The final severing was when our house sold. It was three years before that happened. And when I stepped out of it for the last time, the final chapter of our story was finished.

But in the middle of all of it, God was writing for me a new story. My request of the Lord was for just one man. One man He kept from me by my delay in responding, which I wrote about in this book. Another man came a couple of years later, and I knew in my heart there was nothing good about it, and I had a real sense from the Holy Spirit that there was a "no go" sign in front of it. During that time, I was preparing for an event that we did here in Franklin called Vacation Bible School for Women. I knew it could be a life-changing event for our community, and the pursuit of this man felt like a distraction to God's purpose; so I nipped it in the bud. I ended it with a prayer: "Father, if this isn't from You, I ask You to stop this now." And I never heard from him again.

The Vacation Bible School for Women event was the most powerful thing I've ever done in the past 13 years of ministry. We had women from the highest level of influence in our city to ladies who were still residing in a halfway house for their drug incarcerations or for a number of other reasons. And when it was over, God and I had a conversation on my back porch. I felt like this moment would have to come. But my soul longed to be married again so much, I didn't know that I could ever bring myself to a place of complete surrender. But sitting on my back porch that day with my Bible and a Coke, I began to thank my Father for the VBS experience. And as honestly and sincerely as I could, I said, "Father, if You can make ministry as sweet as this, then I'm okay if it's just me and You for the rest of my life."

This wasn't a planned prayer. It just flowed from the most sincere place inside of me. And it was an odd prayer, because just a few months before I had been praying, walking our usual path, and I was thinking about getting married, and I heard Him say, *Next time, I'll give you away. Since I have fathered you during this season, I want to walk you down the aisle.* I lay on the foyer rug that evening and wept at this statement He spoke to me. Yet even as I lay there weeping, I couldn't help but think how nice it was to be shedding happy tears instead of ones like I had shed in the past.

Then, a couple weeks later, I was reading a book by my friend Rene Gutteridge and Cheryl McKay, called *Never the Bride,* to read for endorsement. The main character helps young men plan proposals while she is desperate to find her own man. Jesus drops by to hang out with her quite often, even though she is the only one who can see Him. At the end of the book He tells her, just like He told me, that He wants to walk her down the aisle. When I got to that part, I wept again, as it so sweetly confirmed what I felt like He had already spoken to me.

So, coming to that place, that day on my back porch, of releasing marriage completely was just a heart thing. I was so connected to my heart in that moment that I knew if ministry could be this sweet and fulfilling, then I could be satisfied with just me and Jesus for the rest of my life. But He had another plan . . .

I started back teaching again and began a piece of the vision that I shared in the book by starting a Bible study for Franklin called The Whole Woman Revolution. In our first semester, I wrote a study on the book of Esther. It was a timely message because it seemed to be a running theme with a great deal of Bible study teachers. One week my counselor, Ken, came and spoke to our ladies. He taught that day on "Letting Go to Love." He was talking about how we have pictures of what we think God needs to bring us. And how we have to let go of the picture in order to get all that God has. My first response was, "Sure am glad I don't have any pictures." I even leaned back in my chair thinking, *I'm glad these ladies get to hear this, because they really need it.*

And that was when the Lord whispered to my heart, *You need to let go of your picture.*

"What picture?"

The picture you have of the man you think I need to bring you.

And immediately I knew I had a picture. And that day I completely surrendered my picture to the Lord.

A few weeks after that moment on my back porch, surrendering my desire for marriage, I felt a huge need to purge. My former husband still had clothes in the closet, and I just felt this deep urgency to get them out. My dad agreed to come up and help me. In the meantime, I had met a wonderful new friend through Ken, named Nate. I had interviewed Nate for my blog, and we had just become instant friends. He asked me to go out with him and a friend of his—a friend who was divorced and had five children. My first reaction was, "No." He said, "Come on. You need guy friends and he needs girl friends." I said, "Well, as long as he knows it is just friends."

So, on a Sunday night, we went to dinner, and that was the night I met Philly Jones. I brought a friend with me as well so I could have some kind of protection. But it apparently wasn't going to be enough. The way the table was set up, Philly and I were able to talk most of the evening, while Berrylin and Nate talked to each other. Every now and then we would interact together, but for the most part, Philly and I spent the dinner getting to know each other.

What he offered me that night was unexpected. He offered me something real. He offered me glimpses into his heart. And the realness of that was very impactful to me. Somewhere in the middle of my fried catfish and grits and his pork chop, I heard the Lord say, *Pay attention. This is the kind of heart of a man I want to give you.* We continued talking, sharing pieces of our stories and having commonality in the fact that we both had been counseling with Ken for a couple of years.

When Nate drove me back to my car later that night, he asked me the dreaded question. The one I was praying wouldn't be asked. "So, what did you think of my friend?"

"He's a really nice guy," was all I offered.

"So, if he asked you out, would you go?" That was the question I was trying to avoid. Because even though I had given up my picture, I couldn't imagine that five children were part of God's picture for me. But there was too much beauty in the heart of that man that I had just encountered not to get to know it better.

"I guess," I said in all but a whisper.

"Denise is going to be my sister-in-law!" Nate hollered in the car, laughing, because he and Philly were like brothers. I slapped him and got out.

The next day, I had an invitation from Philly to go on our first date the next weekend. An invitation I accepted, yet one I had no complete idea would impact my life to the degree to which it has.

Yet there were some things that needed to happen first. My dad came in that day, and the week was all about purging. Purging my old life. I put Philly on the back burner of my mind in order to do what needed to be done. Nate spent the week helping me and my dad, and while we were cleaning out the attic, Nate asked me about some boxes I had kept up there.

"What are those?" he asked.

"Those are my former husband's," I said.

"Well, aren't you going to get them down?"

"No, I thought I'd just do that whenever the house sells."

"Denise, get rid of it. Get it all out."

So we brought everything down. Yet two boxes were filled with our memories. Our wedding album. All of my memorabilia from that time in our lives, and I didn't know how to get rid of it. That was when another friend called.

"Denise, I've had you on my mind this week," and on she began. Near the end of her conversation she said, "You know, when I met my husband, I had some old things from a former boyfriend and I felt like the Lord let me know that I had to clean all of that out before I could completely give my heart away. So I threw it all away." She had no idea that I had just met Philly or that I was cleaning out my former husband's stuff. That was when I knew. I ended the phone call and looked at my dad.

"It's time for it all to go, Dad."

"What do you mean all?" he asked.

"Everything." And together we threw away every picture, every saved napkin, the guest list, everything . . . no remnant remained.

While we were in the middle of the garage sale, another amazing experience happened. A couple of years into our marriage, I had lost the watch my mother had given me on my wedding day. It was heartbreaking, and every time I moved I looked for it and prayed over and over asking God to help me find it. While my dad and I were pricing items for the sale, we came across one of my former husband's suits. It was real expensive, a Calvin Klein. I told Dad, "Surely you can wear this." And I began digging for the size.

I finally stuck my hand into one of the pockets, and pulled out my watch—my watch that I had prayed for years to find, that only a week later would have been gone with that suit. I sat on the floor of the garage and cried. And in that moment, my Father said so many things. First, *I can get to you what I have for you when I'm ready for you to have it.* Second, *Nothing is hidden from me.* Third, *It's time.*

That next Sunday, Philly and I had our first date. It was simply time. A neat moment on that first date came while I was sitting in church that morning. I never text in church. I mean never. But that morning, I had an overwhelming desire for my bike that my former husband had in storage for more than three years. I sent him a text at the end of the service and asked him to bring my bike the next time he came by the house. Later that afternoon, after Philly and I met for lunch, he drove me to his home. He debated on whether to let me come through the garage or the front door. He decided for whatever reason that we would go through the garage. As we walked in, he showed me what he had purchased for he and the kids for Father's Day. Six bikes were lined up side by side . . . God was once again showing me how He loved me in the details. He knew that I would need multiple confirmations to fall in love again, so He loved me with His detailed love as He had for the last two years.

For the rest of that year, Philly and I simply learned each other. Which was funny, because I was so afraid of being relearned. I dreaded it. Yet, I remember one day walking through the grocery store to pick us up something for dinner, and I had this huge smile on my face because I was looking so forward to another date with him to get to know more about him. To learn him. And learn each other we have. We've shared the good and the bad and the ugly pieces of our stories, pieces that will probably never be in print but are a part of what has made us who we are. And do you know what? I enjoyed every minute of the process.

You know what else? He loves my fried chicken, he has read my books and he loves broccoli! In fact, he cooks it so good, I love his broccoli! I've introduced him to my love of movies, to which he replies, "Baby sure likes to be entertained." And he has even endured my love of "garlic and parmesan" salt on my popcorn. He also has (and is) the two things Ken encouraged me to look for. Ken said to look for a man always willing to change. And this is one of the most beautiful pieces about him. He is so quick to look at his own heart before he looks at someone else's. The second thing Ken said was to find someone who brings out the best in me. This man does that beautifully.

I remember for years watching *Diary of a Mad Black Woman,* and each time I would watch it I would be so angry with Helen for not returning to her husband. Yet, one Friday night, I told Philly that I wanted to take him to my favorite hamburger joint and show him my favorite movie. So I took him to downtown Nashville to Rotier's, and that was the night I knew I loved him. At one point, we were laughing and talking and sharing life, with ketchup running down our fingers, and I looked at him and thought, *I love this man. I really love this man.* The next day, he actually told me he loved me for the first time, during the halftime show of a Georgia football game. (Yep, this is my world . . . but we do have a Gamecock flag flying in the bonus room next to the Georgia flag.) But he told me he knew over that hamburger too.

After our burgers, we went back to my house and watched *Diary of a Mad Black Woman;* and for the first time, I knew why Helen didn't go back. Because she found a love that was different, it was honest and real and alive. And I knew that is what God had given me. Philly and I both lived for many years with our hearts shut down. That was our own fault. We own our sin in handing our hearts over to far lesser gods. And we have both worked hard and desperately to get them back. And I believe we have. I believe we have found a sweet place of living that is connected to the very essence and way God created us to be.

Another final piece of this was the sale of my home, something I had spent a long time dreading. Yet I finally came to believe that God was going to keep me there until He moved me to my new home and a new life. On April 10, Philly and I got married, and my heavenly Father walked me down the aisle in front of our closest friends and family; and just a month later, on May 17, after three years on the market, my home closed.

There was nothing left financially when it was over. The savings that had been in my home was gone. But God had proven over and over that He would provide for me, and I was confident that there was no need I would have that He wouldn't provide. But what I can say is that the day I moved out of the house it was into the home of the man that I love. And there was no pain in that

moment. In fact, it was a moment of such excitement and anticipation and, dare I say, confirmation. I got to move into the place
where we have begun to build a life together, and parent together
and make new memories together. And the first home I've ever
decorated! I had never hung a picture before moving into this
home. And now I'm finding I actually enjoy this!

As the house was settled, there was one final meeting with my
former husband. A meeting that was painful and yet necessary. A
meeting where he sent me off into my new life, and I watched as
a life I had known was closed forever. I saw him that day with a
huge level of compassion. And there was and is love in my heart
for him. But it has shifted. It is no longer the kind of love a wife
has for a husband. But more of a love that a mother would have
for a child. And I know that there is an element of him that will
always be with me.

When God brought love back into my life, I began a new phase
of healing as well. In fact, until you get back into relationship with
someone, you don't even know the things left to heal. The insecurities that will surface, the doubts, the questions, the fears, as well
as the desire, the passion, the feeling like a 16-year-old again. All of
that. It just roars to life like a speeding bullet, and you feel like all
you can do is hold on until the crazy thing comes to a stop. But
God has been just as present in the middle of all of that. And He
never stopped tugging me, loving me, guiding me or protecting me.

Becoming the bonus-mom of five children whom I didn't have
the privilege of giving birth to has proven that God is far better at
developing my pictures than I ever could. It does, however, hold its
elements of challenge as well, reminding me that God has one goal
in this life: keeping me perpetually dependant on Him. But the
joys are endless. I'm going to Little League games, football games
and cross-country meets. We love evening bike rides, playing Sorry
and Rummikub, and my girls have taught me how to knit.

They make fun of me because I love to clip coupons, and I remind them why I have to do so. ☺ They also know that I'm addicted to McDonald's Coke, and a few have learned they like it as
well. "How green is my valley" has been added to their repertoire

of sayings, and it's all because they are learning it from me. And I'm learning from them. Their culinary tastes . . . oh my. Their individual hearts. Their gifts and talents, and how each one of them desires to be loved by me.

As I went back through my journals to prepare this book, there have been more moments when I have felt undeservedly blessed. And you know what? I am. I don't deserve any of it. But I'm learning more and more how grateful I am that I don't get what I deserve.

I could write book after book of His detailed love. And that is my greatest desire for you. That you will know God has a detailed love for you. And who knows what books will come out of these next years of raising children and acclimating to this new life? But what I do know is that I will never see God the same way again. And there will never be another person who will have the throne of my heart, except Jesus. I will never hand my heart over again. I will love the man He has given me. Parent the children He has blessed me with. But me and Jesus have a special thing going. He has loved me in my details . . . and I don't want to miss one of His.

My friends, "healing has no playbook," I say that all the time. Don't think that your journey of healing will look like mine. I didn't write this as a formula for healing. I wrote it as a journey I took with God—a God who is always present in grief. I don't want you to take away 10 steps on how to heal correctly. But if some of the things I did sound like something you want to try, have at it. What I do want you to take away is how to invite God into the middle of your pain. How to tell Him your heart's deepest longings and not feel embarrassed. How to claim your stuff, repent of it and then let it go. His net is wide. His grace is inexhaustible. His love is consuming. And His view . . . magnificent.

CLOSING THOUGHTS FROM THE COUNSELOR

By Ken Edwards

Walking through a divorce is one of the most painful experiences you can go through in this difficult, beautiful life. You may not have a choice in the decision to divorce, but you do having a choice in the way you live it out. To put it simply, you can choose to be engaged or check out.

Checking out is easy but expensive. All it requires is a good dose of denial and avoidance. The cost of checking out is your heart. Since the cost is way too high, I'm going to spend my time talking about the freedom that comes from being engaged.

My definition of engagement goes like this: It's the act of being alive to your heart and the heart of God living in the truth of your life as defined by God. You may be thinking that this is hard, and you would be right. You may also be thinking that you can't do this on your own, and once again you would be right. This journey requires the help of God, community and, often, the gifts of a good counselor.

We often avoid engagement because it hurts. It's the pain to which we first need to pay attention, because it leads us to what's broken. By moving toward the pain, we open the door for under-standing what hurt us, seeing what our part was and beginning the process of acceptance and forgiveness. If we choose to avoid, we will become stuck until we deal with it. Going through this journey will force us into a place of dependence on God, because we can't do it successfully on our own.

Since God has created us for relationship, we need to engage our community. Often people who are going through divorce want to hide because they feel shame or some kind of guilt and fear being judged. This kind of isolation is devastating and can easily lead to depression. So get honest with your friends and your church. If they judge you, find new ones. Let them in . . . it won't burden them if you're looking ultimately to God for your strength.

As you're growing in your relationship with God and becoming more open with your community, you may realize that you need more input. If so, seek a godly counselor. Here's the best way to tell if you need a counselor. If you find that you are asking yourself, *I wonder if counseling would help,* that's when you make the call. Ask your friends or pastor for a referral and make an appointment. Make sure your counselor is a good fit by asking yourself a few questions: *Is my counselor really listening to what I'm saying? Do I feel cared for? Is my counselor giving me helpful challenging feedback?*

The last two things I want to mention for your journey is reading and writing. Find good books that will support you, and begin a journal. Reading will give you more than information; it will also give you new ways of looking at yourself and your circumstances. Journaling provides that much-needed space to express yourself. I do it as a form of written prayer.

Flying Solo has provided you a companion for your journey, because Denise has been willing to share the raw intimate pain of her first year of walking through divorce. Read it again and do the homework assignments. Dig in and make the most of your journey. Then buy a copy and give it to a friend or use it in a study. It will open doors of honesty with others who have traveled this path.

Ken Edwards, MDiv, MA

ACKNOWLEDGMENTS

I'm not sure I will ever write a story more personal than this one. So, my acknowledgments are far more personal as well. Divorce doesn't just affect the two people whose lives are severing, but it also affects those who are involved in their immediate world. My family walked with me through this storm in such an intentional way that I could have never made it without them.

To my mom and dad, you loved me so well. You were there when I needed you. You didn't judge me. You loved me. You wept with me. You held me. You comforted me. You were so Jesus to me. I ached that you hurt, but I was so grateful you were there in the middle of such intense pain, and I'm even more grateful that you have been there in the restoring that God has done.

To my sister-in-law Janey. You were there in that season of all things hidden. When the pain couldn't be shared. And you were such a safe place. You prayed with me. You counseled me. You loved me. I don't know what I would have done without you during that time. I'm so grateful that we are family.

To my brother, Darren. You have always been my big brother. But you have more importantly been my friend.

To Damon and Sarah. You babysat me for a good year! Thank you. You never once minded that I was a third wheel to your ride. You just let me hang on for dear life, no matter what that meant, crying, laughing, stealing your baby. You just loved me so well.

To Georgia, you were Aunt Niecy's gift too. You brought life into what seemed like death, and I can't wait to see all that God has for you and that captivating smile and determined personality.

To Hannah, Lauren, Abigail and Jake, some of my favorite times of life are with you. I am so grateful that God made me your Aunt Niecy.

To Deneen, I couldn't have done this without you. Nor would I have wanted to. You were there with me in the toughest moments and in the best moments. And all the years in between. We have shared so much. And few get the opportunity to know friendships like we have.

To Joan, if I could have made a sister, I would have made you. You always believe the best. And you don't care when I'm calling or what I'm saying. You just love me. You are part of my best memories.

To Beth, you have loved me so well. You knew me when I was alive and have watched me come back to life. And you were there when it got so ugly and brought such peace to my heart. What a friend God gave me when He gave me you.

To Packer, my mom away from my mom. Your arms held me so many times, when I couldn't talk for crying, or took care of me when I was sick and my mom couldn't get to me. What a gift you are to me.

To all my friends, who rotated weekends to come and be with me so I wouldn't have to be alone, Lawana, Monica and my second parents Bob and Bobbie, I love you.

To Jamie and Angie George, I'm not sure at times you two knew the gifts you were to me. Jamie, thank you for hearing the call and moving to Nashville. I know it was for so many reasons other than my healing, but God used you in such a precious way in my life. Each week God's word through you was like a balm to my soul. Angie, thank you for your friendship.

To Ken Edwards, what a shepherd and friend you are. You looked at me that first day and let me know that there was hope for me. And I believed you. I really did. And then you walked it out with me, patiently, lovingly and sometimes directly.☺ Thank you for how you so desire to hear God. Because you do. He speaks so beautifully through you. I've told you before that you are one of the most discerning people I know. That only comes through re-lationship. Thank you for how you love God. Because in that, broken people like me get to pick the sweet fruit from that relationship. You are a man among men. And a friend among friends.

To my agent, Greg Daniel, you believed in this when I would have never been willing to put it down on paper. Thank you for encouraging, pressing me and, once again, believing in me.

To Kim Bangs and the team at Regal. Thank you for believing in this manuscript. It has been a privilege working with you.

To my children . . . may the things that God has taught me through my pain and continues to teach me through my dependence on Him be gifts I can pass on to you. I won't always get it right, but I will always desire to. And I am so grateful that God gave me the opportunity to choose you to love. Because I didn't just choose your daddy. I chose you, too.

To my baby. What a gift you are. Painful journeys have a way of allowing us to appreciate good things so much better. I've told you before, but if I had to travel through every piece of that pain to find you, it was worth the trip. Your heart is one of the most beautiful reflections of my Father I've ever encountered. That is why it so stole mine. I look forward to living out life with you. And, like I told you on our wedding day, we may not have 60 years together, but I can assure you I'm going to enjoy every one that we do have.

To my Father . . . what can I say. This entire book is a letter to You. My life is Your story. Thank You for loving me the way You have. Thank You for speaking to me the way You do. Thank You that when all the world tries to cave in around me, You snatch me away, wrap me up and remind me that You've got all of life under control. I love the man You brought me, Father. I do. I'm so grateful for him. But I can assure You, never again will anyone have the throne of my heart but the One who created it. The front seat of my plane is taken now. I have to work a little harder to see You some days now because I no longer have that completely unobstructed view of You. And there was an element of grief to the change in our relationship. But I still see You. And You still make Yourself available anytime. Thank You for the privilege of flying solo . . . with You.

ABOUT THE AUTHOR

From the first pages of her books to the first moments of hearing her speak, people immediately connect with Denise Hildreth Jones's heart of transparency. It is this authentic personal place that she is willing to reveal to the readers of her books, those who attend a Weekend Experience or listen to her Monday Musings or uitlize her Bible Studies.

A graduate of the University of South Carolina's school of journalism, Denise has been writing for more than two decades. A career that began writing for other people eventually led her into the world of fiction and her first novel, *Savannah from Savannah*. Since that first publication, Denise's *Savannah* series, as well as her books *Flies on the Butter* and *The Will of Wisteria,* have been featured in *Southern Living,* hailed as "smart and witty" by the *Library Journal,* and chosen as a Books-a-Million, Faith Point book picks, Women of Faith book club and as a Bronze Medallion Winner in the *Foreword Magazine* Book of the Year contest.

Denise's stories capture humor and heart, and her teaching does the same. She and her husband Philly make their home in Franklin, TN while her five bonus-children are scattered hither-and-yon. She loves Jesus, her family, SEC football, the beach, cold Coca-Cola and a good book herself. She leads Reclaiming Hearts Ministries and you can visit with her anytime at www.reclaiminghearts.org